What Wags the World

Tales of Conscious Awakening

Compiled and edited by

Miriam Knight & Julie Clayton

BOOKS

Winchester, UK
Washington, USA

First published by O-Books, 2014
O-Books is an imprint of John Hunt Publishing Ltd., Laurel House, Station Approach,
Alresford, Hants, SO24 9JH, UK
office1@jhpbooks.net
www.johnhuntpublishing.com

For distributor details and how to order please visit the 'Ordering' section on our website.

Text copyright: Miriam Knight & Julie Clayton 2013

ISBN: 978 1 78279 605 3

A CIP catalogue record for this book is available from the British Library.

Design: Stuart Davies

Printed and bound by CPI Group (UK) Ltd, Croydon, CR0 4YY

We operate a distinctive and ethical publishing philosophy in all
areas of our business, from our global network of authors to
production and worldwide distribution.

CONTENTS

"The best thing for being sad," replied Merlyn, beginning to puff and blow, *"is to learn something. That is the only thing that never fails... Learn why the world wags and what wags it. That is the only thing which the mind can never exhaust, never alienate, never be tortured by, never fear or distrust, and never dream of regretting."*
~ Merlyn, advising the young King Arthur in TH White's *The Once and Future King*

Acknowledgements

Our deepest gratitude goes to the extraordinary men and women who came forward to provide their personal testimonies for this book. While the climate of acceptance toward non-ordinary experiences has been warming steadily, it is nonetheless a great act of generosity, and sometimes courage, to share these very intimate glimpses into the events that profoundly changed their lives.

The contributors to this book are just the tip of the iceberg of authors, filmmakers, and others making seminal contributions to the shift in consciousness that is happening on our planet at this time. We feel privileged to help steward this promising wave of transformation. We also thank our publishers at John Hunt and O-Books, especially Maria Barry, who immediately understood the potential of this volume, and invited us to submit the manuscript. When we read the reports of the publisher's readers, it brought tears to our eyes because... they got it!

We also want to thank our husbands, whose love and support have sustained us through some challenging times.

And finally, we are grateful to Spirit for the grace of being in a position to serve and share the light.

Miriam Knight & Julie Clayton

Foreword

In her introduction to this volume Miriam Knight writes, "An increasing number of people... are having dramatic experiences that call into question the very fundamentals of their assumptions about life... one would say that they are inviting experiences into their life to catapult them into radical change." I should add that this is true of all people who have a modicum of sensitivity to the world around them and are willing to see beyond their nose. They have a perhaps indistinct but usually insistent feeling that something is not right with this world, and that they should be doing something about it. In most cases this is not a sudden call to man the barricades, but a subtle sense that we have lost touch with ourselves, and with the world.

Being aware of this sense is the first step to what Miriam rightly calls an awakening. It is the beginning of waking up to ourselves, and to our place and role in the scheme of things. To the meaning of our life – if there is one. And if we can find it...

In his contribution to this volume Gregg Braden puts it well. He asked himself, "If I died in this moment, if I left the world at this moment and could never come back, and looked at everything that I'd accomplished until now in my life, would I feel complete with my time in this world?" He said that something welled up inside him and screamed, "No." Then he asked, what would it take to be able to say yes? This, for him, became a compass point in life. Nothing was quite the same after that.

This is the experience that catapulted Gregg into radical change; the kind of experience also recounted by the other contributors to this volume. It is the kind of experience we all need. It doesn't necessarily come as a dramatic epiphany; it can also come as a subtle insight and intuition. Its coming to ever more people has become a precondition of human life on this planet – the precondition of setting forth the tenure of a conscious species in an interdependent and delicately balanced web of life.

We are in a race with time. We have launched processes that would lead to the demise of a significant part of the over seven billion of us who now populate the Earth. And if only some of us survive, how would we survive – how could we live? The implications boggle the mind. We are in the same boat – on the same spaceship. We either make it together, or we may not make it at all.

The need is urgent and the opportunity to do something about it is real. We know enough of the threat to know that we have created it, and we must now realize that we can also do something about it. The good news is that we are already doing something about it: some of us are awakening, and awakening is spreading. The question is, is it spreading fast enough? There is a nagging uncertainty whether even awakened people could carry out remedial action in time. We know that many of the processes we have launched reach points of irreversibility, 'tipping points' beyond which there is no return to sustainable conditions. How close are we to these tipping points – and how critical are they? Can we stop the degeneration of the vital balances of the planet's life support systems before they shift into a regime unfavorable to human life? If global warming continues unchecked, will Earth become like Mars: an arid planet inhospitable to life? Inhospitable perhaps not to *all* life, but to the higher forms among which we count ourselves. And global warming is not the only threat to life. We have myriad modes and possibilities to impair our environment and propel ourselves, and other species around us, out of existence.

It is often said that the task is not to forecast the future, but to create it. The forecasts are somber, but they largely neglect the human potential to change it. We do not live in a linear situation. In our current condition even tiny 'butterfly effects' can make a dramatic difference. Are we or can we become the providential butterflies that change the climate, and the climate of change – and change it in time? Can we still create the future?

Our destiny is in our hands. Possibly and hopefully, it is not misplaced in our hands. There is, after all, more to our consciousness than most people realize – 'our' consciousness is not just ours. To paraphrase a passage in *The Prophet*: "Our consciousness is not our consciousness. It is the manifestation of the longing of the cosmos for itself. It comes to us through us but not from us." Khalil Gibran made this remark in regard to children, but it applies to consciousness as well. The cosmos is longing for life and consciousness. On this small but remarkably life- and consciousness-friendly planet we are the species that can live up to this longing.

There is hope. It appears that the kind of experiences recounted by the contributors to this volume are spreading in the world. The kind of questions Miriam and Julie asked them, more and more people are asking of themselves.

The threat is real, but the prospect of overcoming it is less and less somber. This volume makes a real – and at the same time delightful – contribution to making it much less somber still.

Ervin Laszlo
March 2014

Introduction

by Miriam Knight

Doesn't everyone want to know how the world works? For a small child, hopefully, the world is a magical place. Experiencing through all their senses, children probe and explore the cause-and-effect relationships between action and reaction. Their inquisitive minds seek to fit each new experience into an expanding mosaic of how the world works, and how they fit into it. They observe, test limits and create provisional hypotheses as to the nature of reality, filling in the blanks with their imagination.

If the child is very lucky, the adults in their lives may encourage the sense of wonder and the free flight of imagination that are its birthright. Most well-meaning parents, however, feel obliged to prepare the child for life in the 'real world,' and discourage any perceptions or behaviors that are outside their frame of reference. Little by little, in the words of Don Miguel Ruiz, the child is domesticated by the adults in its life so it can live quietly with the herd. The imaginary friends, the knowing of relationships that endured in different forms through many lifetimes, the ability to see energies, heal others or know the future are denied validity and eventually are lost, along with an innocent sense of joy of life and a certain light in their eyes.

The thing is, after one has gone through school, gotten married, had children, had a career, and taken stock, there is sometimes a nagging sense of emptiness. There is a return to the deeper questions of what's it all about? What is the purpose of my life? Why is the happiness that is supposed to come with material possessions, with security, with power and influence in the world so elusive?

An increasing number of people in this position are having

4

dramatic experiences that call into question the very fundamentals of their assumptions about life. In terms made popular
by New Thought and the New Age, one would say that they are
inviting experiences into their life to catapult them into radical
change. Examples of these precipitating events include:
catastrophic accidents, loss of job, severe illness, a near-death
experience, a dark night of the soul, visions of otherworldly
beings or simply a deep knowing that penetrates the depths of
the soul.

Often, such individuals go through a phase of questioning
their own sanity, but the knowing persists and grows. As they
surrender to this knowing, there emerges a sense of connection
to something greater, a mysterious or mystical source of which
they feel a part. People give it many different names: source,
spirit, great mystery, the Tao, God.

Some may interpret their revelation within the context of
their existing religious traditions, and this results in a deepening
of their faith. For others it exposes a world that transcends
conventional religion, a world of connected inhabitants sharing a
communal spiritual experience. It imbues them with a sense of
deep connection to the source of all being, to God, to love, and
sets them on a path of service. Their perspective of what is
important in life is radically shifted, and the material world no
longer holds much charm.

The revelations and personal shifts that people have
described run the gamut from profound understandings of the
nature of the forces underpinning the very fabric of physical
reality, to the ability to visualize the interior of human bodies
and having the capacity to change their molecular structure and
create miraculous healings, to the ability to hear and even see
beings in other dimensions, and convey their messages to
friends, loved ones, and the world at large.

It is my hope that the tales presented here will remind our
readers of experiences in their own life that may have been

5

dismissed as fantasy or coincidence, and give them permission to reconnect with the magic of the universe. It is time to reclaim our birthright as joyous, limitless souls.

Introduction

by Julie Clayton

My Tale

Like some of the authors' stories in these pages, my life so far has been more of an agglomeration of 'aha' moments rather than having a single identifiable turning point. Throughout the years I have occasionally felt slightly envious of others who could point to a defining moment in which they had an epiphany, or the metaphorical light bulb went on, and their life trajectory reset its course toward their authentic work in the world. On the other hand, I don't envy those for whom this shift was catalyzed by a traumatic event, and I'm certainly not wishing to invite that into my life.

I have, however, had a lifelong intimacy with my dreams. Since childhood my dreams have been equally as significant and 'real' as my waking world. In fact, my first childhood memory isn't a birthday party, or a doll, or our family pooch, but a dream. Without any effort on my part, the veils between dreaming and waking have always been thin, like cheesecloth, and my dreams regularly filter through into my waking world (and vice versa). From this innate trait I realized a fundamental principle about the nature of reality at an early age: consciousness is a continuum – although, I did not have an objective awareness of this, it simply was my experience.

Dreams are one way we can expand our preset ideas about what is possible. In adulthood, I have deliberately used my dream state to explore the elasticity and multidimensionality of consciousness – my own and cosmic – joyously tinkering each night in the 'workshop of conscious evolution.' In forging this self-intimacy, I have discovered that dreams respond to my desire to become more conscious of the universal energies at work and play in my life.

One notable *waking* dream occurred about twenty years ago, when I was driving on a southern California frontage road that paralleled the freeway, going about 45 miles an hour. A friend and her three-year-old daughter were in the car with me. The road was oddly empty, other than a single car coming toward me – on my side of the road! I looked, not so much visually but psychically, into the eyes of the oncoming driver and I knew that this person was 'absent.' I could tell that her rational mind was not engaged or present. So I swiftly calculated that I should stay in my lane, hoping/expecting that she would 'wake up' and realize her mistake, and instinctively swerve back to the correct side of the road. As our cars came closer and closer, I could see that the driver was still unaware of her surroundings, and we were going to crash.

And in that moment I completely surrendered. I was calm and totally accepting of what was about to occur, and that I was probably going to die. I raised my hands from the steering wheel and said to god or anyone who might be listening, "I surrender." And I bowed my head and closed my eyes. And in the next moment, I looked up to see our cars miss by inches. It truly was as if a divine finger had gently pushed the other car just out of the way. I pulled over to collect myself and it was then that the adrenalin rushed through my body. I looked in the rear view mirror and the car had vanished!

More recently, I had a profound nocturnal dream three weeks after my mum's passing, which had the rare quality that comes only with 'big dreams' – when the dream seems so vibrant and realistic. The brief backstory is that my mother and I shared a close and loving relationship: I was blessed to be her caregiver in my home for the last three years of her life as she gradually succumbed to Alzheimer's, and thanks to the assistance of home hospice, I was with her when she exhaled her last breath.

In the dream I am sitting in my kitchen with my sister, and

hearing a noise from my mum's room, I go to investigate. I find my mum sitting up in bed, animated and chattering away. I think to myself that this is strange because she's dead, but ask her if she wants any food, or anything to drink, as I would have usually done. She doesn't speak to me directly, but gets up and wanders around the room, and I see that she doesn't have on any pajama bottoms. I go to retrieve some pajamas from her drawer, and then remember that I gave away all of her clothes after she passed. Once again I think it's a bit strange, because I know she's dead, yet here she is seemingly quite alive. But since I am open-minded, I just go along with the dream.

My mum is back in bed and I sit on the edge of the bed, facing her. Suddenly, an inch-wide arc of blue-white light emerges from my third eye, and pours into her open mouth and down her throat! At first I am seeing this from behind my eyes, and then I shift perspectives and see the scene and myself objectively, as if someone else were watching it. After a while, this arc of light/energy stops flowing and my mother leans over toward the opposite side of the bed, as if she were picking something up from the floor. Looking through my own eyes again, I can see her naked back and a large eye-shaped hole that goes deep inside of her. I see that she is hollow inside... but then realize that the 'empty space' inside her is streaming with beautiful, golden-light sunbeams. I awaken, thrilled to have had what I consider to be her final gift – a glimpse of the integral nature of reality, and her incorporation into it... into the All That Is.

My Insight

Like a subterranean river, these events and the many other 'intuitive' moments of my life have given, and continue to give, shape and form to my experience of reality itself. They have carved out an abiding, slow-burning passion as a lifelong student, writer, and teacher of what I call "all things consciousness" – so much so, that I even pursued a Master's degree in Consciousness Studies. My continuing self-directed studies into the nature of consciousness and metaphysical principles has highlighted how inadequate words are to express anomalous experiences – and yet, we must continually give them voice and engage in this conversation if we are to arrive at any favorable agreement about what it means to be human and thus how to proceed toward positive outcomes for the human species.

I do know that the universe is far greater and more mysterious than anyone can apprehend, or can even imagine, at this stage of our conscious development. And that my dabbling in this multi-layered mystery through dreams and intuitive faculties brings me a little closer to realizing what it means to be part of the mind and the heart of the universe. It changes my psyche, and this transformation carries into the world, giving life profound meaning for me.

My Message

We are asleep to a lot of things in the world. But in this Age of Conscious Evolution humankind is stirring into wakefulness: the time has come for each of us to expand the nature of his or her own consciousness to include a more profound – *and humane* – version of reality. The contributors to this collection of transformative tales demonstrate that such conscious expansion is already occurring more commonly than is generally acknowledged, and that there is no singular or 'right' path for this awakening.

The experience of life is a perpetual movement of self-realization. A baby pushes at its boundaries and explores its world, and with each new piece of information its boundaries grow to include that awareness. Conscious evolution follows this same process. We continually explore our bubble of reality until it expands to the edges of its boundaries – and then, like cells populating, it divides into more bubbles, over and again. And sometimes during this process, our reality bubble is penetrated with an activation of awakening that transforms our entire view of the world. And our place within it.

Allan Hunter

My Tale

Was there a particular event or experience that was a turning point in your life and somehow changed your view of the nature of reality?

Yes, there was, and I think many people have such turning points, but when the initial shock has worn off they tend to slip back and forget about them, which is sort of what happened to me. My turning point was a form of near-death experience, in that I nearly died, but it wasn't the sort of thing you typically read about where someone has the experience of bright white lights and meets the Almighty. My experience was relatively dramatic, and it did change my life, but it wasn't until several years later that I really looked at this event to try to understand it.

I had been working in England with some of the most disturbed adolescents in the country. There were many tensions in both my work and my personal life, and I developed a severe lung infection that wouldn't go away. The good old British National Health Service was doing its best to heal me, but hadn't a clue why I was getting worse. So I went to an acupuncturist, which was very daring in Britain in the 1980s, and the dear lady took one look at me and immediately brought me a cup of tea, because when I staggered into the office I was turning blue from lack of oxygen. It took 45 minutes to warm my body up enough so that she could take a pulse. Years later, when I asked myself what had really happened there on that acupuncturist's table, I realized that I had given up hope of being alive. I had reached the point of total surrender. And that moment of total surrender to whatever is in the universe, I think, allowed it to step in and say, "You don't have to try. You don't have to be the best at anything. You don't have to impress anyone." I still choke up when I try to talk about it. This nameless, voiceless awareness seemed to convey to me, "You are held and that's all you need to know." It was like being held in the palm of the creator. It was surrender, and I'm so glad that I did it without knowing I was doing it, because total surrender is not something you consciously do – it's something you allow.

My Insight

What insight did you have as a result and how did that affect what you do now?

The initial feeling was one of gratitude that I was alive, but then I realized that gratitude is just the first step in a process that really can reorganize our lives, whether we've had a dramatic experience or not.

And then what followed was the second of five steps, or insights, that can lead any of us towards self-awareness. This second step was a firm sense of humility. Humility always leads us to a different relationship with what we might call ego – my damaged, needy self that wanted to be reassured all the time. That was the tipping point, because I think that led me to the third insight, which is when you feel humble and look around at the world, you see that it's incredibly beautiful. It is when we appreciate that sense of beauty that we come closer to a sense of loving the world we are in and we step back to our primal, most powerful and most vulnerable selves, which is what I call the discovery of innocence. This is the fourth insight.

From that place of innocence we begin to rediscover that yes, we are all connected, and so we have to rethink our relationship to the rest of creation. And so the final insight is seeing one's place in nature and realizing that, yes, I'm here to do a job, I'm here to serve. If that's the case, and that's where the authentic part of me can flourish, then I must find out all the ways that I can serve this planet. I keep reminding myself every day that I'm here to do something constructive, and so to 'get on with it.'

My Message

What message would you like to leave with the reader?

Practicing gratitude is a wonderful place to begin, but don't stop there. If you stop there, it's a bit like visiting Paris and having lunch at Maxim's and then leaving immediately afterwards without seeing the rest of the city. It just doesn't make much sense. If you've had a marvelous, challenging experience like this, you have to process it thoroughly. In the middle of this series of events I was left without my health, without any money, without a job, and eventually without loved ones around me. It upset every bit of my life, but this was absolutely necessary; otherwise, I couldn't have seen what I needed to see to rebuild my life on a foundation that was not about proving myself. If we don't know this is what's happening we will simply rebuild ourselves on the shaky foundations that have already let us down. By contrast, if we stay with the gratitude, feel the sense of humility, and move towards that wonderful sense of beauty, then I think we can rebuild ourselves on much firmer foundations – foundations that are not built on the opinions of others or on the demands of the wounded ego-self.

Bio

Allan Hunter is a full professor of Literature at Curry College, MA, a counselor, and has a doctoral degree in literature from Oxford University. British by birth, he traveled extensively in Europe, Africa, and India before settling in Boston, Massachusetts. He has spent his life exploring the intersection of literature, ancient wisdom, and the ways of the heart. His studies have led him to uncover the extraordinary power that exists within certain texts, ancient and modern, and to find the ways we can access that power in our own lives.

His workshops use writing and story to reach a place of deeper understanding and peace. His books include: **Stories We Need to Know; Life Passages; The Six Archetypes of Love; Princes, Frogs and Ugly Sisters: The Healing Power of The Grimm**

Brothers' Tales; The Path of Synchronicity; Spiritual Hunger; Write Your Memoir; and his most recent book is **Gratitude and Beyond** – *an exploration of how gratitude is just the beginning of the journey of self-discovery.*

Allan's website: www.allanhunter.net

Anita Moorjani

My Tale

Was there a particular event or experience that was a turning point in your life and somehow changed your view of the nature of reality?

Absolutely! It was my near-death experience that came as a result of end-stage cancer. When my organs finally started to shut down after four years of dealing with cancer, I entered a coma, which my doctors felt would be my final hours. But in actuality what I entered was the state of incredible clarity and understanding, where everything made sense. And I understood – for the first time – the meaning of life, the meaning of *my* life. I understood how I came to be lying in that hospital bed at that moment in time. I understood what caused my cancer. It just all really made sense. And at that point I was faced with the decision of whether I wanted to come back into life or to continue in the other realm.

At first I wanted to stay in the other realm, but it felt like I was being encouraged to come back into life. My father was there, in that other realm, and I felt he was trying to tell me that it was not my time and I should go back. And then I got a sense that there were still some gifts waiting for me on this side, and I knew the truth about returning: that my body would fully and rapidly heal from cancer. It was almost like I wanted to come back just to prove that was true.

And I understood that heaven was not a place – it's a state. Now that I knew *this* truth, I knew I could bring this (heaven-like) state with me. This state isn't about being in the other realm or in this realm – you either are it or you're not, and it doesn't matter which realm you're in. I realized that I could re-create this state here on earth, and that was now my purpose, to come back here and re-create it here. And so I did choose to come back, and the cancer healed very rapidly. What I've been doing every day since is to just live my life from that state, which I touched during the near-death experience.

My Insight

What insight did you have as a result and how did that affect what you do now?

First of all, I want to say that the world we have created is, for some reason, completely upside down and back to front from what we intended it to be. In the other realm it felt like we never intended for it to be this way, so I have no idea why we got it so wrong. It feels like this world was created by the blind leading the blind, and we cannot get it more wrong than it is. Yet, I also feel that we come here knowing who we are, and knowing how powerful we are when we are born: we know how amazing and magnificent we are. It's as if we get thrown into this system that brainwashes us into forgetting. It brainwashes us into believing that we need to prove ourselves, compete with others, to prove that we're better than everyone else. Because of this societal conditioning, we are constantly sending ourselves the message that we aren't deserving, we're not worthy.

Similarly, we are constantly sending our bodies the message that we don't have the capacity to heal and that we need to go to somebody else, who's 'qualified' to heal us. Or, that we don't have the capacity to find our own answers, and must turn to someone outside who is more qualified to tell us what to do, and so on. And so we become conditioned into losing self-confidence and grow up feeling inadequate, unworthy, and unlovable, which often leads to dysfunctional relationships in adulthood. And then we spend the rest of our lives going to self-help seminars and reading self-help books in order to rediscover what we were born with in the first place, but spent the first half of our lives forgetting.

Nothing else will work in your life unless you love yourself. It's not about how other people treat us; it's about how we treat ourselves. You just have to love yourself. Really, it's that simple, and that was the insight which saved my life.

My Message

What message you would like to leave with the reader?

I tell people, "You already are everything that you are trying to attain." You already know the truth within you. And I make it very, very, very simple. The only thing that I ask people to do – that they need to relearn to do – is to learn to love yourself again. The biggest thing that erodes away as we go into this system that we've created is our own love and self-respect, and our value for ourselves. We start giving our power away; we start believing that we need to work hard at being lovable, at being accepted, at being liked and needing to fit in, and so on, but the way other people treat us is a reflection of how we treat ourselves.

So, in the spirit of keeping it simple, what I tell people is that the most important thing is to find your joy again. Every morning just ask yourself, "What would make me happy?" Because every single person on the planet deserves to be happy. And when you start to allow yourself to find your joy or when you start to recognize what makes you happy, that goes hand-in-hand with so many things. It goes hand-in-hand with learning who you are, with loving yourself; and you start losing your fear. Because when we don't love ourselves we are very fearful. And when we're fearful there is no room in our life for love. Conversely, when we love ourselves there's no room in our life for fear.

The secret ingredient is very simple: it's just saying every day, "Am I doing this because I'm fearful of the consequences, or am I doing this because I love myself, I value myself, and I love my life?" It's as simple as that. Every day that's the only question we have to ask ourselves.

Bio

Anita Moorjani was born in Singapore of Indian parents, moved to

Hong Kong at the age of two, and has lived in Hong Kong most of her life. Because of her background and British education, she is multilingual and, from the age of two, grew up speaking English, Cantonese and two Indian dialects simultaneously, and later learned French at school. She had been working in the corporate field for many years.

In April of 2002, Anita was diagnosed with terminal cancer. On February 2, 2006, doctors told her family she was just hours away from death. It was at this point that she 'crossed over' and then returned again into this world with a clearer understanding of her life and purpose on earth. This understanding subsequently led to a total recovery of her health.

Her fascinating and moving near-death experience in early 2006 has tremendously changed her perspective on life. Her work is now ingrained with the depths and insights she gained while in the other realm. She works on the premise that our inner world (consciousness) is our primary reality, and if our internal state is healthy and strong, then our external world will align itself and fall into place as a result. She is the embodiment of the truth that we all have the inner power and wisdom to overcome even life's most adverse situations, as she is the living proof of this possibility. She is the author of **Dying to Be Me: My Journey from Cancer, to Near Death, to True Healing**.

Anita's website: www.anitamoorjani.com

Barbara Berger

My Tale

Was there a particular event or experience that was a turning point in your life and somehow changed your understanding of the nature of reality?

Yes, I think one of the most mind-boggling is an experience I had when I was 20 years old, when my husband Steve and I were on the run because of the Vietnam War. I grew up in Bethesda, Maryland, and by the time I was 18 I ran away from home. At that time in the 1960s I was underage and so I couldn't be legally independent. Since my parents had the police after me, I married Steve who was 21 years old because he then became my legal guardian.

I felt joyously free at first, but shortly after that Steve was drafted to go to Vietnam. We were opposed to the war, and to escape the draft we left the United States. (This made matters worse with my family since my father was a former high-ranking military man who had worked at the Pentagon.) That time, in the early 60s, was also when everybody started taking drugs. We had been all over the world and ended up in Mexico where I had a very bad drug trip and I freaked out completely. After I came down from that traumatic experience we were taking a train to Mexico City. It was an all-night ride in a crowded third-class car, with this overwhelming press of humanity, families and chickens and goats all squeezed together in a very small space. Then finally people fell asleep right where they sat. And suddenly in the stillness, I had an awe-inspiring revelation. At the time I knew nothing about spirituality. I had never heard of awakening and had no understanding of the nature of reality or consciousness or mind, or any of the things that I know today. The combination of the exhausting journey, the drama, the drugs, the death of the ego; the whole thing just opened me like a flower.

I actually wrote down the details of my experience in my first published book *The Journey* (1968), and the language I used as a non-spiritual 20-year-old really demonstrates the universality of the awakening experience. I'm still in awe of it today, after studying spirituality for my whole life, that I described it so well. As I look back, I now understand that I was experiencing divine bliss consciousness or cosmic consciousness. It was such an expanded state of awareness. It was a paradigm shift from the linear to the nonlinear; perceiving everything all at once. It was beyond languaging and explanation. I saw that reality is all happening now and in that expanded state of awareness I was everyone and everything. I had somehow touched upon that exalted state of heightened awareness when your whole existence becomes blissful radiance. In that state, there was nothing to seek and nothing to do and I knew I was finally home.

My Insight

What insight did you have as a result and how did that affect what you do now?

It's interesting. I had no context for it at that time and no one to help me understand what I had just experienced, so I didn't know what had happened to me other than it felt so extremely blissful and satisfying. Since that was during the tumultuous time of the Vietnam War, we ended up getting political asylum in Sweden. It was the time of the youth rebellion and the psyche-delic movement so I continued experimenting with mind-expanding drugs and moved to Copenhagen, Denmark, which was a hotbed of change. I even traveled overland to the East with the wave of European hippies – seeking all the time to find that blissful state again.

My motivation in life, already starting back then, was to find a way out of suffering: first at the social-political level, and then through the whole alternative movement with food and Macrobiotics. I've always been a teacher, but it was first after the health food days in the 1970s that I really started to understand that transformation and awakening had something to do with the mind and consciousness. It was only when I studied the science of mind and Buddhism and traditional spirituality that I started to have words and understanding of the things that I had previously experienced.

With greater awakening and clarity, I also began to experience dark nights of the soul. I discovered that the agony and the ecstasy go together. But the more understanding I get, the more I realize that anguish is often a catalyst for awakening.

My Message
What message you would like to leave with the reader?

It's not a linear path to awakening for most people, and it's a process, not a one-time event, even for people who have had a powerful awakening experience or several like I've had. I've noticed that spiritual seekers are often naïve about that. They think, "I'm going to get it and be saved!" I think a more realistic attitude to all of this soul evolution is that challenges, anguish, trauma – they're often the catalysts for spiritual awakening. It's been a great comfort to me, anyway, that I've heard this from other people. Then the challenge is how to integrate the awakening experience into your being. You get these glimpses – and then what are you going to do with it? We still have to deal with our daily lives, so the integration of these different elements can be very challenging.

Part of the problem, I think, is the confusion between the Absolute and the relative. When we have a powerful awakening experience and taste the amazing bliss and peace – that is a taste of the Absolute. But in our daily life, that is the relative world of changing phenomena; when we look for this kind of absolute satisfaction in our relative experiences like our job or our partner or our body, we are bound to be disappointed and suffer.

The importance of an awakening experience is it gives us a glimpse of who/what we really are, but we need to find the right balance between the everyday psychological aspects of our lives and the greater spiritual reality in order to have a satisfying life. The challenge for many of us today having these awakening experiences is how we integrate all of this and use it to realize our fullest potential and be of service.

Bio

Barbara Berger has been a seeker all her life – and all of Barbara's books are based on her life work, which has always been to try to find a way out of suffering. Her quest to ease suffering has led Barbara to explore many different pathways and approaches – mental, physical, metaphysical, psychological and spiritual. After leaving the US in the mid-60s in protest against the Vietnam War and settling in Scandinavia, Barbara continued her quest with a passionate interest in the science of the mind, the nature of consciousness, metaphysics, and finally traditional spirituality and psychology.

To date, Barbara has written 15 self-empowerment books documenting and presenting the tools and insights she has discovered over the years on her quest. Her books include the international bestseller **The Road to Power / Fast Food for the Soul** *(30 languages);* **Mental Technology / Software for Your Hardware (The Mental Laws)** *(8 languages);* **The Spiritual Pathway** *(5 languages);* **Are You Happy Now? 10 Ways to Live a Happy Life** *(17 languages); and* **The Awakening Human Being: A Guide to the Power of Mind** *(5 languages). In all her books, Barbara explores and explains the incredible power of mind and how we can use this power wisely to live happy lives right now, regardless of outer events and circumstances.*

Barbara was born and grew up in the United States but today lives and works in Copenhagen, Denmark.

Barbara's website: www.beamteam.com

Bernie Siegel, MD

My Tale

Was there a particular event or experience that was a turning point in your life and somehow changed your view of the nature of reality?

There were many. I keep saying my life should be a movie because nothing 'normal' happens, but let me start with the simplest one. I was attending the workshop that I thought was for doctors, run by Dr. Carl Simonton, to help empower cancer patients by using imagery and things of that sort. Such 'alternative' methods were not routinely accepted in the medical profession at the time, but it still blew my mind that I was the only doctor there out of 125 people.

In the workshop we were directed to do some guided imagery. Even for me that seemed like craziness: I went there to learn something, not to close my eyes. But I did shut my eyes because I knew the facilitator was watching me from the stage. Now, I happen to be an artist, and when you're a visual person and you close your eyes, boy do you see things. In one guided imagery we were encouraged to meet an inner guide – and I met a man named George who had a big beard, a strange cap on his head, and beautiful white robes. I really was expecting Jesus or Moses, because I'm a doctor and I thought I'd really get some classy guide; but no, this odd-looking guy shows up and says he's "George."

Some time later I was speaking at Mercy Center, a spiritual center run by Catholic nuns. At some point I realized that I was no longer giving the lecture. I was talking, but I wasn't following my notes or saying what I expected to say. Words just came pouring out, and I let them flow because what I was saying seemed good. A woman approached me after the talk and said, "There was a man standing in front of you for the entire lecture, so I drew his picture for you." Well, it was a picture of George, with his big beard, cap, and robes.

A year or two later, at that same place, I spoke at the funeral of a Christian friend of mine. After the funeral when everyone else had left, my friend, who is a healer and intuitive asked me, "Bernie, are you Jewish?" I replied, "Why are you asking me that – because I spoke at a Christian funeral?" She replied, "No, there's a man standing next to you, a Rabbi." And she described George again, and that's when I understood his outfit, and the hat he was wearing, and everything else. And that was a totally mystical experience.

Now, I don't live my life based on what I believe. I live based on what I experience. If I experience it then I believe it. When I was age four, I was home with a cold and there were carpenters working in the house. In those days they'd put the nails in their mouth as they were working, and then take them out one at a time to hammer into the wood. So, I took my toy telephone apart and put the pieces in my mouth, like the carpenters. I inhaled a piece and began choking to death, unable to call for help. It was one of the most painful things that I'd ever experienced in my life, because my body – my diaphragm and all those muscles – was desperately working to get air in. Then, just as suddenly, I was free of pain.

I was in the air over my bed, looking down at the boy who was dying. The experience was incredible! I was free of pain, out of my body. I had no notion of near-death experience – and it never occurred to me to wonder how I could see or think since I wasn't in my body. But the thoughts going through my head were that being dead was more interesting and exciting than being alive. I mean it, I made the choice: I wanted to be dead! It was so fascinating and interesting.

I also felt that my being dead would be hurtful for my parents, and I was sorry for that, but it was just too good an experience to not stay there in that pain-free, exciting place. And then the boy on the bed had a seizure, vomited, and all the pieces came out: it was as if someone had performed a Heimlich maneuver. He took a deep breath and the only way I can describe what happened next is that it was like getting sucked into a vacuum. I was back in his body again. And that's why I feel I have an Angel. My mother came in not long after that, but I never got to talk to her about what happened.

One final story, although there are many, many more I could tell you. Years ago I attended one of Elisabeth Kübler-Ross's workshops – she became a close friend – and I had to draw a picture. She looked at me and said, "What are you covering up?" She continued, "You made a mountain with snow." I replied, "What does that have to do with anything? And she said, "Bernie, the page is white." You took a white crayon and added a layer of white to a white page. So what are you covering up?" And this was a huge 'wow' moment: in the drawing were all my feelings, things that I was hiding and had buried, but symbolically they needed to be revealed.

That inspired me to go back to the hospital with crayons to get my patients to draw. I began saying to patients, "Draw a picture, tell me your dreams." The stories, and what they revealed about their body and the wise choices for treatment, were something coming from inside the patient. Those drawings and the imagery exercises that I began to bring into my practice changed my view of the nature of life.

My Insight

What insight did you have as a result and how did that affect what you do now?

It's all these things and more that keep intertwining. It's almost like knitting your life. One thing leads to another, and when you're willing to be open to that intuitive stuff it will change your life, and maybe even heal you. The key that I try to share with people is like the story of the ugly duckling who looks at his reflection in a still pond and realizes that he is a swan. But it has to be a still pond. If you quiet your mind, you'll know what you need to know.

Joseph Campbell said that Nietzsche told us to "love your fate." What he meant was when you're going through hell, ask yourself, "What have I learned from this experience?" And that has helped me. So when I don't like what's happening in my behavior, I say, "What can I learn from this?" And basically the answer is always, "Compassion." So then you say to yourself, "How can I be compassionate towards this other person in their experience?" Then you're helping yourself and them.

My Message

What message would you like to leave with the reader?

Don't let others impose a life on you. Let your heart make up your mind, not other people. When you make mommy and daddy happy doing what they want, you'll lose your life. Live your authentic life and not one that others impose on you. And when you can love your life and love your body and not see it as a threat, but love it, it literally gets a chemical message saying you love life, so it does everything it can to save your life.

The opposite of love is indifference and abuse and rejection. So if you grew up with those things you need to re-parent yourself, and you rebirth yourself, you become a new person. I tell people to think of themselves as a blank canvas – you are a work in progress. Act and behave as if you are the person you want to become. You know, if you draw blood from actors, their immune function and stress hormone levels change depending on whether they are in a comedy or a tragedy. So, find a life coach. Act and behave as though you are the person you want to become, and rehearse and practice. And how you give love to the world is up to you. And then look for common themes.

We need to become one family, and to realize that we're all the same color inside, even if on the outside we're different so that we can recognize each other. But how are we going to save the planet? By recognizing how we are all one family and that there's nothing to fight about. That's what the world needs to do – become family.

Bio

Bernie Siegel is an American writer and retired pediatric surgeon, who writes on the relationship between the patient and the healing process as it manifests throughout one's life. He is the author of 13 books, including his first and best-selling book, **Love, Medicine and Miracles** *(1986).* More recent titles include **365 Prescriptions for the Soul;** *and* **A Book of Miracles – Inspiring True Stories of Healing, Gratitude, and Love;** *and his latest is* **The Art of Healing,** *revealing through drawings and his experience the message.*

Bernie was born in Brooklyn, NY, and attended Colgate University and Cornell University Medical College. He graduated with honors and holds membership in two scholastic honor societies, Phi Beta Kappa and Alpha Omega Alpha. He trained to become a surgeon at Yale New Haven Hospital, West Haven Veteran's Hospital and the Children's Hospital of Pittsburgh. In 1989, Bernie retired from Yale as an Assistant Clinical Professor of General and Pediatric Surgery to speak to patients, their families and caregivers.

In May 2011, Bernie was honored by the Watkins Review of London, England, as one of the Top 20 Spiritually Influential Living People on the Planet. He continues to break new ground in the field of healing, supporting changes in medical education to 'humanize' medical practice.

Bernie's website: www.berniesiegelmd.com

Cyndi Dale

My Tale

Was there a particular event or experience that was a turning point in your life and somehow changed your view of the nature of reality?

There certainly was: I'd even say there were a couple of them. One occurred when I was just a small child around four years old. I started to wake up to what people would now call extrasensory or paranormal perception. Of course, I thought these perceptions were normal because I was a kid and I thought them neat.

I became conscious that there were colors around people, that those colors would change when they were in different moods; so, Mom might turn red when she was mad and Dad would turn a funky yellow before he was going to drink his martinis, but when they were getting along there would be a pink color around them both. The colors were so interesting I started to more consciously pay attention to things people might consider supernatural. Besides seeing colors, I could hear voices, which I thought was perfectly normal.

For instance, one evening in bed I could see the hallway door to my parents' room and I heard visitors in the house. I knew they were hobos, though I don't even know how I knew the word. Most likely I had heard my parents talk about hobos in relation to the railroad tracks behind our house. At any rate, I heard the hobos making breakfast in our house. They were chatting and I could hear the bacon frying. Then I heard them chitchatting and leave, and the only thought I had in my mind at that point was that I hadn't heard the water running. They had left the dishes. I knew that Mom was going to be really mad. I woke my parents and they were really upset with me because there weren't any dishes in the sink. I was told that I was just making things up.

My intuitive senses remained fairly open until another really big life-changing event that was on the dark side, which affected me in a negative way. My family system really eroded over the next few years and became quite negative and painful – full of alcoholism and abuse. I looked at my parents when I was about 12 and I said I'm going to die now. I'm done! What are you going to say when your kid says that, especially if you don't want to believe them? I became violently ill and lost about 20 pounds within two or three days, and ended up leaving my body one night. I was done. I was very willful and as I started to go up toward the heavens, I heard a voice say, "You have got to go back." And I said, "No!"

The voice said, "Well you've not done anything yet." And I said, "So what?" Well, from my point of view, I was totally ignored and 'smooshed' back into my body. I remember a hand forcing me down, but kindly. However, I wasn't happy and decided that though I would 'be here,' I wouldn't 'be present.' My intuitive gifts completely closed down and over the next few years I developed a number of really challenging disorders – obsessive-compulsive, anorexia, bulimia.

During that time, I did not let myself access spirit or think spiritually and I became very challenged emotionally. I only started to change when I went to therapy at age 19 or 20. The therapist looked at me and said, "You know, based on your story, you aren't only codependent, you're actually quite psychic." In some ways that sentence probably changed my life more than anything, because it set me on a journey to figure out what she meant. I had never heard the word 'psychic' except in connection with the occult, or warnings from my family that only the devil spawn see images or pictures, or talk to spirits.

Her words emboldened me in a very positive way to start exploring that world just beyond this world, beyond the one we live in. After that, whenever I could, I started traveling abroad to study with shamans and healers, and going to the places and the lands where hearing voices, talking to the dead, and doing healing work were normal. So it was that series of events that led to a diehard family systems therapist encouraging me to find out what being psychic meant to me. I've had many other wonderful events that have opened me up and helped me access spirit more and use my capabilities more, but I think those earlier ones were the seeds.

My Insight

What insight did you have as a result and how did that affect what you do now?

I think that the major insight it gave me is that we have choices, and we need to exercise this power to become something better than what we are. In fact, it's up to us to develop a level of consciousness that allows us to perceive the choices that we have. As a kid, maybe very unconsciously, I made a choice to use my gifts and to be at one with them. I chose to believe in things that other people were telling me weren't real or true. In my teen years I made a choice to shut myself off and down, primarily because of wounding, pain, and resentment. I have a lot of compassion for myself for only being able to perceive darkness when there was still light, at some level. Later I made another choice, this time to open myself up again.

The choice of deciding what we're going to do with our wounds, what we're going to do with who we are, how we're going to choose to believe in this universe and in other people, is our own. We must have divine and eternal forgiveness for the times we have made the choices that darken our senses. We have to forgive ourselves, which is only possible if we understand the compelling urge to survive, cope, and fit in. Because life can be so hard, I use that phrase, 'we can choose' from a place of grace, not shame. We can't shame ourselves for the choices we've made that haven't been so good.

The nature of the psychic gift isn't actually complicated. It involves picking up on energy that moves. We can pick up on good energy and bad energy, harmful or helpful energy, and we can do good things or bad things with it. So again, there are lots of choice points there. In deciding to figure out what being psychic meant for me, it was inevitable that I chose to make it my profession. Remember that statement, 'we teach what we need to learn'? My path was to figure out what being psychic meant for me; inevitably this pursuit has become something that I could use to help others. I've had a wonderful career, but I don't really think I would consciously go back and want to choose it, to be really honest. It's hard to be an energy healer and an intuitive. You're dealing with invisible energies and you don't know what they are all the time. You're working with people's attitudes, which aren't always so accepting, and you're encountering people's fears. It's not like it's been a golden bridge to peacefulness and ease.

I remember when my son was 14. You know, teenagers just want to be normal and he didn't want a mother like me. His dad was a vet with a PhD who specialized in animal swine management. So my son looked at me and he said, "Now, what am I supposed to tell my friends my parents do – my mom's a bloody psychic and my dad's a pig doctor!" I was filled with guilt.

I laugh now because 20 or 30 years into my journey I'm popular, and I go to parties and people say, "Oh, that's so cool!" And I'm thinking, *where were you 20 years ago?* And people even say, "I really want to do what you do when I grow up." And I say, "Really?" So it became what defined me, but in a really interesting way it's not what defines me either. Do you know what I mean? We are so much more than what we do for a living, even though the choice to become a professional intuitive shaped my life.

My Message

What message would you like to leave with the reader?

I think I can summarize it by saying that there is only beauty in YOU. No matter what stage of life you're in, you are such a beautiful being. Think of the butterfly; sometimes you might feel that you're a little more like a caterpillar – like you're just clawing your way along; or you're like larva, new at everything; or you're in the cocoon – the dark night of the soul. But you – all of us – no matter what stage we are in, are simply beautiful creatures... your gifts are beautiful, your failings are beautiful, your past is beautiful, even your scars are beautiful. Everything – every choice – has taught you how to use your wings and enables you to fly.

Bio

Cyndi Dale has been a natural intuitive since she was young, and is an internationally renowned author, speaker, healer, and business consultant. Her books to-date includes the bestseller, **The Subtle Body: An Encyclopedia of Your Energetic Anatomy**, *published by Sounds True.*

The Subtle Body *has garnered over 100 five-star reviews on Amazon.com and continually sells in the 2,000th place, leading millions of books. It has also won four internationally recognized Publisher's Awards. Her other world-renowned books include* **New Chakra Healing**, *now published in over twelve languages and revised in an all new edition;* **The Complete Book of Chakra Healing; Advanced Chakra Healing: Energy Mapping on the Four Pathways; Everyday Clairvoyant; Kundalini: Divine Energy, Divine Life; Attracting Prosperity through the Chakras; Advanced Chakra Healing: Heart Disease; Advanced Chakra Healing: Cancer: The Four Pathways Approach; The Littlest Christmas Star; Illuminating the Afterlife; Togetherness; The Intuition Guidebook; Energetic Boundaries; Beyond Soul Mates;** *and the newly-released,* **The Subtle Body Practice Manual.**

Cyndi has presented seminars and workshops all around the world, and has been trained in several different healing modalities, including shamanism, intuitive healing, energy healing, family of origin therapy, therapeutic touch, the Lakota way and faith healing and holds a fourth degree mastership in Reiki. She taught business ethics at the University of Minnesota, served as a public relations consultant to 3M and Tonka, and has been honored in "Who's Who in American Business," "The American Women of Noteworthy Achievement," and the "International Association of Business."

On a daily basis, Cyndi works with clients and groups, serving as an intuitive coach and an energy healer. Clients are commonly referred by professionals, including psychiatrists, medical doctors, and therapists. She continues to hone her ability to help people discover their essential selves so that they can make healthy and positive changes in their lives.

Cyndi's website: www.cyndidale.com

David Bennett

My Tale

Was there a particular event or experience that was a turning point in your life and somehow changed your view of the nature of reality?

I'd have to say I had three very powerful experiences that were turning points in my life. The first was a near-death experience, the second was a spiritually transformative experience, and the third was stage IV lung cancer that metastasized into my spine, causing it to collapse. The unique setting was that each experience had spiritual implications that built upon the next, leading me toward awakening. The near-death experience left me feeling alone and isolated because I had no one to share it with at that time.

The near-death experience happened when I was a commercial diver. It was a total paradigm shift and it really rocked my world because as an engineer I saw things pretty much as black and white. And then I had this incredible experience in the light that just did not fit into my reality at that time. It took a period of integration to bring that experience into who I am. What happened was that I drowned in a very stormy sea with 25 foot waves – a very ferocious night. Being tossed and tumbled by those waves was the most violence I had ever experienced in my entire life. I couldn't fight it, and I drowned.

At first I was in absolute darkness, but I found it comforting because I'd just come from all this violence, so the darkness wasn't frightening to me. It was absolute, and it felt like I wasn't alone. I really didn't feel alone and I was comfortable. Then I saw this light. It came toward me and, as it did, I was greeted by three fragments of the light that welcomed me. They welcomed me home, and eventually a dozen fragments of this light were with me and we went into the light together. We experienced my life there: I had a total life review.

During the review I did not perceive any judgment. You know how we talk about the end of our lives, that we face our judgment day? It was interesting – the judgment I did feel came from myself. I brought the judgment, but my soul family didn't judge me. As we reviewed my life, they were loving me and supporting me through it. It was as if I had to overcome and let go of my life, let go of all of IT in order to learn through this experience. Throughout this life review everything was crystal clear, until I started to see some things that I didn't relate to in my life. I started seeing my future! That was not as clear; it was almost like I saw this core path of potentials that my life could take. And if I deviated off the path, it wasn't quite as clear. But if I stayed with this core, then it was reasonably clear what was going to happen. And then the light spoke to me and told me it was not my time – that I must return. And I argued with the light, but the light spoke to me one more time and it said, "No, you must return. You have a purpose."

And because I was connected to this greater consciousness that was so much more than just myself, I understood that purpose and I agreed to come back. And then I found myself back in my body after a miraculous resuscitation at sea.

My Insight

What insight did you have as a result and how did that affect what you do now?

Well, I have to group all these experiences together and say that they showed me how interconnected and interdependent we are in this physical life, as well as our spiritual lives – the spiritual lives that we lead. I now understand how important it is to live with honesty and love in this moment and to do the best that I can in each moment, and that way I'm walking the path towards the brightest possible future.

I realized that the basic human quality of opening up and helping each other is within each of us. That spark of goodness is always there. It's our unconditional instinct. You know what to do, and you do it. Now, with that realization we are called to service, and service to the world in whatever way we can contribute to the betterment of humanity. My path is turned to helping others experience or integrate their experiences, so they can become whole. Also I'm working on my next book to share my reflections with the world in such a way that it allows everyone to find their own path to spiritual awakening.

My Message
What message would you like to leave with the reader?

I would say to allow the seeds of love to brighten your life and to carry you toward an un-knowable future that's filled with unlimited potential. When we allow love to strengthen our being toward living with a passionate and compassionate heart, which naturally leads us to heartfelt actions, then we are truly living our purpose. At our core is love. Each of us has felt it and longed for it in our hearts, yet our minds don't understand love – this invisible force that calls us. The love of our core being tells us to accept ourselves, to love ourselves, and to give love naturally in everything that we do. This love is at the core of the universe and this love is awakened consciousness. The true shift in our consciousness is toward loving intention. That will carry over into our work, our play, and our total living. This is a common shared purpose for all of us.

Bio

Coauthor of **Voyage of Purpose: Spiritual Wisdom from Near-Death back to Life***, published by Findhorn Press, October 2011, David is a spiritual activist who invokes empowerment with grounded and practical spirituality. He is a champion of the soul and a catalyst for transformation.*

A public speaker and teacher, David has lectured at the International Conference of IANDS (International Association for

Near-Death Studies) and shared his inspirational message at numerous groups across the country including Lillydale. Now in remission and retired/disabled David's passion includes working with experiencers and cancer survivors to integrate their Spiritually Transformative Experiences. He has consulted for both radio and television, including Oprah and Dr. Oz as an NDE resource, appearances including being filmed for NBC national news, PBS, and Coast to Coast AM *with George Noory, and many radio shows. David's articles appear in various magazines, blogs and papers: you can find David's daily reflections of living an empowered life on Twitter and Facebook.*

David's websites: www.DharmaTalks.com
www.VoyageOfPurpose.com

Dianne Collins

My Tale

Was there a particular event or experience that was a turning point in your life and somehow changed your view of the nature of reality?

I've always been a seeker, and I had a sequence of events through my life that were all interconnected. I always saw what I would call a great divide between ordinary life and the underlying great wisdom of all mastery traditions. I realized that there was a disconnect between what we aspired to be as humans and how we actually behaved – not attuned to unity consciousness, and lacking compassion. Even as a teenager I looked for how the world could change and realized that it could only happen by changing myself.

One memorable experience occurred when I was on a sailboat with my boyfriend in the Bahamas. I was in the exquisite aquamarine water and had asked him to throw me a snorkel mask, which he did, but when I went to catch it, the buckle sliced my finger deeply. I climbed back on the boat, emotionally shaken, and wrapped my tiny finger in a huge towel. I was surrounded by a throng of people offering help and opinions, when one woman pushed forward, grabbed me around the shoulders, and shooed everyone away. I hadn't even noticed her before, but she said to me, "Now I want you to close your eyes, and imagine this clear water coming up from the sea, washing your whole body." She takes me through this 5-minute meditation, saying things like, "imagine a light coming down..." I'm going along with her, but I'm also wondering how she knew I'd even be responsive to this kind of help. By now my finger had been put in a smaller wrap, and she says, "OK, open your eyes."

I opened my eyes and looked down at my finger and unwrapped it. It was already healing! She looked at me and said, "You give it lip service, but you lack faith." I realized in that moment the extraordinary faculties of the mind that I hadn't been fully using, like intent and intuition. I saw clearly the relevance of the quantum field with its infinite possibility, and thought that there must be a way to awaken consciousness to this greater reality through an understanding of the new science. This planted the seed of what I now call *QuantumThink®*, the system of thinking I developed which is that bridge from just 'knowing' the wisdom to actually *living* it – from just giving it lip service to having a visceral understanding alive in every moment.

My Insight

What insight did you have as a result and how did that affect what you do now?

First of all, I realized that this experience with this woman was not an accident. I had just read *Autobiography of a Yogi* the week before, and intellectually accepted the experiences Yogananda wrote about. But when this woman showed me how we literally can transform our experience of reality, Yogananda's words penetrated, and I 'got it.' It's not a matter of belief based on evidence, it is based on inner knowing. It is living and embodying the wisdom of the creative power of mind. In a sense I always knew this, but this experience was a profound deepening of my knowing.

Transformation is not a one-time event. We can read the same thing and listen to the same talk over and over, and each time – because we are continuously evolving – it will penetrate deeper. We will get it at a deeper and deeper level. The consciousness keeps expanding and we become established in that state.

My mission, as it evolved from that experience, was how do I become a catalyst for others to connect to that aspect of themselves – so we are walking-talking embodiments of the greater multidimensional reality.

My Message

Is there a message you would like to leave with the reader?

I have three messages:

We are, literally, interconnected and interdependent.

Live the wisdom. Live the wisdom of the great spiritual traditions, and live your wisdom as an individual adding to the collective. Really connect to who you are. In this time of great transition, this shift to a higher evolutionary stage for humanity, it's our duty to get in touch with what gifts we have been given that enable us to live our unique purpose. See the patterns in the totality of your story that will give you the clues to living this purpose, which may take many different expressions throughout your life.

When you master your mind you master your life. We have this faculty of consciousness that we create with, that we shape life with. It is incumbent upon us to learn what these faculties of mind are – what I call the five natural faculties of mind: intent, intuition, subtle energy, resonance, and meditation. Not the psychology of mind but the incredible power of consciousness with which we are divinely endowed. When we do this we can literally live masterful lives. When you master your mind you master your life.

Bio

Dianne Collins is the author of the 6-time award-winning bestseller **Do You QuantumThink? New Thinking That Will Rock Your World**. *A former Fortune 100 corporate manager, Dianne is a much sought-after TV and radio guest and consultant to business executives and entrepreneurs. She has an extraordinary gift of originality and the ability to express complex universal subjects in clear and powerful ways that people can instantly resonate with. Building on her lifelong studies in philosophy, psychology, physics and metaphysics, yoga, and business, Dianne's QuantumThink® system is an original synthesis of the principles of quantum science and universal laws applied as modern* *practical wisdom to make life better and more joyful.*

Dianne's website: www.diannecollins.com

Eva Herr

My Tale

Was there a particular event or experience that was a turning point in your life and somehow changed your view of the nature of reality?

There was a very profound moment in my life, although I suspect that the knowing it opened in me was always there. As a child I was very empathetic to the world around me, and as I grew older that empathy didn't go away, it just got hidden in the egoism of life.

As an adult, some really bad things happened to me where I had a very dark night of the soul. My child was kidnapped, my father died, I got pregnant, and I lost my job all within the space of 30 days. A few years later, I went to bed and had a dream, or what I perceived to be a near-death-like experience without having to die. I actually perceived that I went to the other side. Whether I did or not, I can never really know, but when I woke up the next morning I knew things that I didn't know before I went to bed.

In that experience, my father came to me and took me on a journey to the other side. I asked, "What are you doing here, you're dead." And he said, "Sometimes when you don't get to tend to something before you die, God lets you come back. I didn't get to tell you that I loved you, and I didn't raise you right." I said, "What you mean you didn't raise me right?" I'd been raised in the Christian religion so I believed in a burning hell at that time. The next morning I no longer believed in a burning hell and nothing had changed except that I had this dreamlike experience. When I awoke the next morning I understood that everything is really perspective... everything is simply cohesive forms of thought. I understood that there is only one energy. That there is no matter on the quantum level – reality as we know it is really holographic, for there is no such thing as

43

matter. Everything that is, is right here, right now. It was an instantaneous epiphany... I get it! It was a knowing as real as I knew my own name – even more so because not only did I *know* the truth in the experience, but I *felt* the truth in the experience. It was a life-changing experience.

Prior to that, quite frankly, I really wasn't a nice person to be around. I had turned away from the tender places of my childhood and grown into something hard and narcissistic. So when this unusual experience happened it was almost like the striking of a match and the flame illuminated who I really was. Afterwards I realized that I am *everything* that is, and everything that is, is me. So, as I treat humanity I treat myself, for energy does not stop, it just changes forms. It is a proven fact in physics. There was also a feeling that came with the new realization. I don't mean to be inappropriate, but the best way I can describe this is like an orgasm – but not a sexual thing. I felt as if I was plugged into an electric socket and literally vibrated with bliss. For about six months following, I felt like I was walking about two feet off the ground. I suspect this happens because the body's electromagnetic field changes.

The event happened in 1993, and since that time I've learned that the best piece of advice I can give is to simply be. Stop thinking about what was or what might be... simply BE. We create today what we live in the years to come. I have to admit, I've been talking about this for years, but only within the last six months did I *really* get it.

My Insight

What insight did you have as a result and how did that affect what you do now?

You never start playing a game to lose... at least, I never have. You go out there to win. Whether it's playing a tennis match or a game of Monopoly, one usually plays to win. My perspective is that we choose certain life experiences in order to facilitate the life lessons we need to learn. I can assure you that we pick a life wherein we will ultimately win. It's how we play the game that determines how much fun we have, or not. We forget that. It's illogical to think that we would intentionally choose a life in which we ultimately lose.

It is important to note that one must define exactly 'what is losing?' Feeling bad is *not* losing. The worst thing that can happen is that we die, and if we die we go back to the non-dual state. (Suicide is not the same and is not a pain-free escape.) It is the spiritual growth of the soul that is the ultimate goal of the game! It is possible to evolve the soul without pain. If you can *truly* learn lessons through others, you can avoid a significant portion of the pain typically suffered in physical reality. In order to do so you must learn to observe a situation from a 365-degree perspective. In other words, observe the situation from the perspective of all involved, not just yours.

I've had lots of things happen in my life (and yes, I did get my child back) – but I finally realized that if I just watch these things occurring and don't fixate on them, they don't take over my life. It's like watching a movie and the events pass by without any result or any emotion. So I'm able to be happy with life as it is because I don't latch on. Imagine that you are sitting in a movie theatre watching a movie. You can run up on the stage and shout, dance around and flail your arms around all you want, but you are not going to change the movie. You change your personal experience in that moment... but the movie is what it is.

I went to bed one night being this miserably unhappy human being and the next morning I woke up in bliss. I also woke up with a very profound gift of medical intuition. Ever since that night, I have been able to detect illness in others for years into the future. I can actually perceive very subtle symptoms that an individual is suffering at the moment. Symptoms that are so subtle one would not even recognize them as symptoms... until I explain the relevance and then one would say, *Aha! That makes so much sense.* The experience also catalyzed another major shift: it took me away from the narcissism of Eva Herr – you know, the 'What can you do for me?' attitude, to 'Oh my God, what can I do for humanity?' All I care about now, other than my family, is humanity. I went from being completely egotistical and material-istic to not caring about anything except humanity. I care about helping people get on a path where they can find hope and happiness and contribute to making the world a better place. I care about teaching people how to early detect and prevent disease. I care about teaching people how to use food as medicine.

I had a massive heart attack last year and I decided to walk my talk. So now I use food as medicine, and if you saw me today you'd never know that I had a massive heart attack a short while ago. I feel better than I've ever felt in my life. I'm happier than I've ever been in my life, and all I'm doing is eating whole foods and not minding other people's business. Not trying to tell other people how to live their lives. We all know Gandhi's message, "Be the change that you want to see in the world." Start with you. You can't fix the world; you can only fix you on the inside. And the way to do that is by being still and listening because, if you do, amazing things *will* happen.

So, I practice silence… the frequency of manifestation is silence. The more time you spend in silence with positive thoughts and positive images that you want in your life the more likely they are to happen.

My Message

What message you would like to leave with the reader?

My message is to treat everyone the way you want to be treated. Care about another as much as you care about yourself because you *are* that person. Hug your children, don't text your children. Put your arms around them – it makes a difference. Our children are the ones who are going to bring the world around for the future, and there are many, many children coming into the world today that are awake. By the time they reach six or seven they are different, but the world doesn't recognize them as being different. The world sees them as being problem children. They're not problem children. They often see things that you don't see and hear things that you don't hear. Nurture them and nurture yourself.

Visualization is the most powerful practice I can encourage people to do. It etches into physical reality one molecule at a time. But be very specific about what you visualize, otherwise the pieces form but they cast out into the universe. They scatter much like pieces of a puzzle blowing in the wind and then you have to go find them and put them together. Your vision needs to be whole and complete.

Bio

Eva Herr is the author of **Agape, The Intent of the Soul** *and* **Consciousness – Bridging the Gap Between Conventional Science and the New Science of Quantum Mechanics**. *She is a featured luminary on Gail Lynne Goodwin's "Inspire Me Today," and Inspire Me Today's "Ask A Luminary," a qualified trial expert, medical intuitive, radio personality and magazine columnist. She is an active advocate for holistic and nutritional health as it relates to early detection and prevention of disease, mood disorders, and addictions. She lives with her family in Atlanta, Georgia.*

Eva's website: www.evaherr.com

Foster Gamble

My Tale

Was there a particular event or experience that was a turning point in your life and somehow changed your view of the nature of reality?

Yes, there have been a number of such incidents, but I would say that the main one for me is what was depicted in our film, *THRIVE*. I was riding in the school bus when I was 14 years old, gazing out of the window watching the light flickering through the trees. Suddenly, I began seeing a full-blown vision of a whirlpool vortex of light that then turned into a solar system with the sun in the center and the planets going around the outside; and then it turned into an atom with the nucleus at the center and the electrons going around the outside. Then, somehow, I got a whole body feeling that I too was that same torus pattern – somewhere about halfway in scale between the tiny atom and the solar system. The message that I got was that this was the fundamental pattern of the energy of the universe and that I was to find out more about it. And I have spent the rest of my life doing that.

I would add also a bookend experience. At age twenty-three I discovered the non-violent martial art of aikido. When I started practicing aikido I realized that my task as a human being was to learn to blend with the energy pattern of the torus that I had seen earlier *at every single level* – from the physical to the mental to the emotional, to the spiritual, interpersonal, environmental. It was a matter of recognizing, and then dancing with the wholeness of the flow of energy in this toroidal pattern. That realization sent me in a clear direction.

My Insight

What insight did you have as a result and how did that affect what you do now?

I think the main insight was that aligning with the torus is the key to thriving. I began looking at my own purpose in life, and what has become clearer and clearer to me is that my purpose is to learn more and more in every way to thrive, which is aligning with that torus pattern, and then to share what I learn with others who are interested. So, my learning has taken on many, many different forms, and so has my sharing with others: the most recent has been creating *THRIVE*, and the movement that's come out of that film.

You asked me if I see this torus as both a physical manifestation and as a metaphor. That's a wonderful question because one of the things that the torus taught me is that this whole notion of physical is an illusion. If we look at what we think of as purely physical, our bodies for example, we see that the body is made up of cells, which are made up of molecules, which are made up of atoms – which are made up of 99% empty space! But it turns out that even the atoms are just whirlpools in a continuous a sea of infinite energy, consciousness and love.

We tend to think of ourselves as physical beings, but really we're just a very intelligent agglomeration of toroidal vortices that expresses its consciousness through the plane that we call physical. Because our senses are attached to our physical form (our sense of smell, our hearing, and such), they are tuned for our survival to the frequencies that we call the physical world. But really we are, by definition, not mere physical beings because our consciousness precedes the physical. It shapes and organizes and then guides the path of these whirlpools that we call our bodies. And by the way, every cell in our body has been replaced within the last seven years, but we can stop and notice that what we call ourselves is still here. And that's beyond the physical consciousness. So yes, the torus is a wonderful template for how a healthy system sustains itself in the so-called physical universe; but it's also, as you say, a metaphor or an icon for wholeness itself.

When I look, as we did in *THRIVE*, at the numerous serious

problems in the world that are literally threatening life as we know it, it turns out as far as I can tell that the solutions to all of those problems comes back to recognizing wholeness. Whether it's honoring and stewarding the wholeness of an ecosystem, or the wholeness of our health, or the wholeness of the seed, or the wholeness of a complete, honest communication, or the wholeness of an honest money system: at every level, the reason we're not thriving is that we have allowed natural systems to be broken down from their wholeness. And really all we need to do is to understand the natural wholeness and allow the systems to go back to that state and stay aligned, in order to survive and thrive.

My Message

What message would you like to leave with the reader?

If I could pass on one message succinctly, it would be to encourage people to pay attention. Because any moment can be an extraordinary one that absolutely changes the quality of your life. And as you tune in to that awareness, to open your eyes and open your mind and really consider freshly what you're seeing. Then open your heart so you can hear your own inner guidance as to how to respond to what you're seeing. And when you hear that clear voice of inner guidance then I encourage you to stand up and speak up and link with others in creating a thriving world. As we say in our theme song, "We already have what it takes to thrive."

Bio

Foster Gamble is President and Co-founder with his wife, Kimberly, of Clear Compass Media, which produced the documentary **THRIVE: What On Earth Will It Take?** *Weaving together breakthroughs in science, consciousness and activism, THRIVE offers real solutions, empowering us with unprecedented and bold strategies for reclaiming our lives and our future.*

Previously, Foster was CEO of MindCenter Corporation and an instructor in the non-violent martial art of Aikido. He was the on-screen host for the PBS documentary **Aikido – The Way of Harmony**. *Foster created three training programs: Interaction Dynamics, LifeBalance, and Zonesport, which he has delivered for corporations, schools and sports teams throughout the country.*

Foster's exploration of 'living geometry' came to fruition in 1997 when he co-convened the Sequoia Symposium, *a multi-disciplinary scientific think tank exploring perspectives on "Unification Theory." There, the primary energy patterning of the universe was clarified and recognized as a blueprint for designing sustainable technologies and social systems. This discovery represents the convergence of science and the evolution of consciousness that Foster set out to explore after his initial numinous vision at age 14, and is the 'code' that is featured in* **THRIVE** *and on this website.*

Foster lives in California with his wife Kimberly Carter Gamble.

Foster's website: www.thrivemovement.com

Frank DeMarco

My Tale

Was there a particular event or experience that was a turning point in your life and somehow changed your view of the nature of reality?

First I was going to be a politician or statesman and then I was going to be a writer, but many things happened. In 1987 I had just come back from the chiropractor after seeing X-rays of my ribs and spine, which showed them to be frosted with arthritis. During that time I couldn't stand, or sit, or do anything without extreme pain. I was depressed by the thought that at the ripe old age of 40 my life was over.

I didn't watch television as a rule, but that night my wife very uncharacteristically suggested I watch the Shirley MacLaine special *Out on a Limb*. And I, rather uncharacteristically, thought that was a good idea.

I sat for three hours watching the first part of this special. Although I wasn't interested in her love affairs, some of the spiritual and paranormal things she revealed were fascinating! And when I stood up at 11 pm to turn the television off, I realized my back didn't hurt – at all! So of course, I watched the second half the following night, and my back still didn't hurt. I was living in the Norfolk area at the time, and Shirley MacLaine's first seminar was being given that Saturday and Sunday in Virginia Beach. So I immediately signed up, thinking that this was a really a big message I was being given. And by the way, I had to get X-rayed many years later and there's no sign of arthritis. It just went as fast as it had come on, and that really got my attention.

Since I was a journalist, I wrote a 2,000-word article about the MacLaine seminar that appeared in the Sunday paper the following week, one that wasn't dismissive or scornful. This was unusual for a mainstream journalist, so by that afternoon everyone in the Virginia Beach/Norfolk area New Age community knew my name. It actually didn't do my career with the paper any good, but as a result I was invited to a party several months later. At the party I met Bob Friedman, and he and I went on to found Hampton Roads a few years later. So all of that came from what seemed like an incurable ailment that just suddenly went away while watching the Shirley MacLaine special. If this were someone else's story, I would have some reservations about believing it. But since I was there and it happened to me, I don't have a whole lot of choice.

My Insight

What insight did you have as a result and how did that affect what you do now?

I have another turning point that is perhaps more relevant. Because of that Shirley MacLaine special, and Bob and I getting together, eventually I wound up doing the Gateway program at the Monroe Institute in December 1992. I spent the entire week of the program desperately wanting to access psychic abilities and powers that I had read about and which I believed that other people had. There was a woman in the program who really interested me, although not in a romantic way. She seemed important somehow, and later I realized – although I don't think of past lives in the same way that most people do in general – that it was a form of past life connection. On the last day of the course, I seemed to have to choose between still trying to get the abilities and the insights that I was looking for or helping her. At this point I can't even remember what the nature of that conflict was. But I decided that it was more important to help her even though I was giving up what I really wanted. As a result of that decision, I got what I wanted, because that's when I learned that psychic ability doesn't come from the head, which is where I had been looking for it, but it comes from the heart. And that was a huge turning point.

Once you realize that psychic ability comes from the heart and not from the head, gradually over time you learn that, in fact, there are only two forces: love and fear. Another way of looking at this would be to say that one force is expansion toward others, and removing the barriers between yourself; and the other is contraction – establishing barriers or reinforcing them, and saying, "No, this far and no further." I think in duality they are both necessary, but it would be natural that love is the way to access your psychic abilities because that's how you destroy the barriers.

I knew then that the path of love and of destroying the illusion of separation between people is the path I wanted to take. When you see it that way, then love doesn't become this nice warm fuzzy abstraction – it is the truth about life. Eventually I learned that the inside of things and the outside of things are the same, even though reality perceived through our emotions and intuition can seem very different from that perceived through our senses.

Now, look at what this understanding does. If everything that seemingly is external to you is actually intimately connected with who or what you are, it shows you this is really true that there are no problems that are not also opportunities. One way of looking at it is to say that before my life started I chose all the potential things I might want to work on. And therefore any problem I experience in my life is the result of those choices. What this tells me is that who I am and what I am is vastly more than what I'm conscious of. And the only way we become conscious of what was unconscious in ourselves is through the world – through other people, through events, and the like. So therefore, all those events and people become an opportunity to become more aware of something in ourselves that we don't know about. Carl Jung said, "Until you make the unconscious conscious it will rule your life and you will call it fate." And I think there's hardly anything more profound than that. Once you eliminate the victimhood, once you eliminate the anger at other people, once you eliminate the sense that you're in an out-of-control situation, everything changes. Everything becomes much more fluid and much more joyous, and you can live in trust.

My Message

What message you would like to leave with the reader?

I was complaining to a friend of mine that I wished I had done this or that at Hampton Roads. And finally he said to me, "More than most people I know, you trust the present and you trust the future. But when you say things like I wish I had… or, I shouldn't have… you are mistrusting the past that brought you to where you are in the present." So that's my long-winded answer to your question. When you learn that you really can live in trust and when you learn that anything and anybody who happens to you is an opportunity for you to learn more of yourself, which will therefore make you freer, then there's nothing to fear.

In duality, fear has its place as long as it's appropriate to the situation. But once you know that love is the way to expand into the world and connect with other people and reduce your isolation; and once you know that the inside and the outside are the same thing and that everything around you is an opportunity, then what else can you ask? What else do you need?

Bio

Frank DeMarco was co-founder and, for 16 years, Chief Editor of Hampton Roads Publishing Company, Inc. He is the author of five non-fiction books and two novels, including **The Cosmic Internet: Explanations from the Other Side**.

His past and current thinking may be found on his blog, which discusses "Everyday explorations into our Extraordinary Potential," and on Facebook, where he is frank.demarco.10.

Frank's blogsite:
www.hologrambooks.com/hologrambooksblog

Gaetano Vivo

My Tale

Was there a particular event or experience that was a turning point in your life and somehow changed your view of the nature of reality?

I am a Reiki Master teacher, trained in America, and a few years ago I turned away from my way of teaching Reiki. I just felt that it was no longer fulfilling my heart. It may only have been in my mind, because people were still benefiting from my healing abilities, but something really stopped me because I felt that this was not helping any more. So during a meditation while I was teaching the last segment of my 2-year Reiki 3 class in Naples, Italy, I went into a spontaneous channeling experience where this group of beautiful beings began talking to me. They were little angels, like children, who told me they were called the Angels of Transparency.

I believe these angels came to me at that point in my life because I was going through some deep personal turmoil. I had become aware of certain things that needed to be addressed, including the realization that inside me there was this deeply unhappy little boy. So it was like inner child work, and these angels helped me to go through this very difficult time.

This huge group of little angels appearing like that was profoundly life shocking. I don't think I was ready to see such a multitude of angels. In fact I don't think I was ready to be starting to work again. Mind you, I'd been working with Reiki for 10–15 years, and the last thing I wanted to do was to start over again. But, I don't believe that a spiritual teacher can go on teaching without an inner journey, or inner validation, so I started working with these Angels. I left Italy and moved back to England, because I needed to be alone. I spent a lot of time in my little garden, which has a beautiful, elemental kind of energy, and started working with the Angels of Transparency. They were teaching me things and telling me what to do with my life and were helping me heal my inner child.

I should add that since I was four years old I would see an Angel coming into my bedroom, and he would actually take me away to see surreal worlds. Later when I became a much more spiritual person, he presented himself to me and told me that he was the Archangel Michael, that he is one of my guardian angels and that he has been working with me ever since I was born.

My Insight

What insight did you have as a result and how did that affect what you do now?

The Angels were talking about love: giving love, receiving love. The Angels have taught me that it is very important to be centered, to be completely and utterly able to go inside and to work with yourself. First of all, go and work with your inner child. Try to love him or her. A lot of people have this very bad relationship with their inner child. They do not know how to nurture him, they do not know why they abandoned him or rejected him so often in their lives.

The Angels were telling me that the reality is that we are called to be in service, yes, but we need to be able to heal ourselves first in order that we can actually give other people as much love as is needed. It is like taking people by the hand, step-by-step. I had this very beautiful metaphor of humanity being like a newborn child still suckling from its mother. Newborns are born blind, and don't yet know about the world around them. They need to be nurtured and supported as they are taken step-by-step into the new reality.

Over the course of a few years of daily meditation and practice, I have developed the skills and a new way to help people heal their inner child. This is all in my book, *Messages from the Angels of Transparency*. The work continues and last week I had another book published in Italy as well, which is like a continuation of last year's book. It's called *Ama e Basta*, which means 'just love,' and which I have written with the help of my great friend, Mr. Francesco Italia. Love is the most important thing. People fear love, but one should never be scared of this emotion. If you know how to love, and if you know how to teach people how to love then that is the most important thing.

My Message

What message would you like to leave with the reader?

The best talent that each one of us has is God. You should never be afraid of your talents and how to express them.

Love is the most important emotion, love governs everything; without it you cannot function in the world.

Mother Theresa used to say, "You cannot do great things, you can only do small things with great love."

While writing my last book, *Just Love*, the Angels wanted to give us an insight about fear and love. Here is what they said:

Fear is a child that hides himself, it is a journey with no coming back. Stop for a moment and ask that child to proudly smile. Ask that journey to show you the way to bring you back home. Do you hear this vibration? This vibrant flow that brings tears to your eyes? This is who I am, this is my love for you. It is the love of the universe. Love that forgives and purifies. Love that rescues, love that waits, love that comforts. The love of the mother, the love of heaven and earth. The love of those who are no longer with us but look upon us, guiding us. Do you fear love? Do you fear that this love is too much for you or not at all? Love has no space, no time. Love is here now, it is for you and you can protect it. Take care of it but do not try to understand it. Love is enough. Don't ask anything else of yourself because no fear, no wounds can resist this love. This love is mine, is yours, it belongs to this magnificent universe that smiles at you.

Gather your tears like love drops and use them to heal whom you will meet on your path. Fill them with joy, pure joy, joy of rejoicing. Receive your gifts without asking why. Your gift is big and does not know fear. Simply give yourself. This is who I am. Don't be scared of me.

Let me guide you and ask me to assist you. Because I love everything about you.

We have so many beautiful things to do together, lots and lots of people to meet, we have many souls to touch. They are waiting for you. We are waiting for you. God is with you and he blesses everything.

Just love...

Bio

Healer, speaker and author, Italian born Gaetano Vivo works in the UK, Italy, US and more recently Asia. As well as being a fully qualified and advanced practitioner of Reiki, he is a member of the Complementary Medical Association of Great Britain, the International Council of Holistic Therapies, the International Association of Reiki Professionals, and a member of the Institute of Noetic Sciences.

Reiki is one of many healing therapies he practices; others include Vibrational Psychic Surgery, Crystal Therapy and Karuna Reiki Treatments. In addition to treating clients from all walks of life, Gaetano also instructs students in the art of Reiki. Gaetano, himself, became a Reiki Master following a turning point in his life. He ran a bookshop (The Metaphysical Centre) and people commented on how relaxed they felt in his presence. He initially experienced Reiki from a ten-minute taster session and from that point on it was as though an enlightened path had been laid before him and he decided to learn more about this ancient healing art. When his training was sufficiently advanced he began offering his staff treatments and then set up his clinic.

Gaetano is the author of several books, including **Messages from the Angels of Transparency**.

Gaetano's websites: www.gaetanovivo.co.uk
www.gaetanovivo.com
www.amaebasta.it

Gary Douglas

My Tale

Was there a particular event or experience that was a turning point in your life and somehow changed your view of the nature of reality?

I've always been different. Throughout my life I felt like I didn't fit in or belong. I tried every church, culture, religion, group I could possibly find to see where I belonged, but I never got there.

I had a strange experience, which ended up in my trying to become a channel. I was living in a house in Santa Barbara where long ago there had been Indians who had overwintered there. I woke up in the middle of the night and saw this Indian standing in my room, but only his top half was visible. I was having a fit, wondering what on earth this apparition was. Finally he just disappeared. After that experience I began looking into parapsychology and metaphysics – anything that would explain this bizarre experience of seeing a ghost. As I searched the world for what else might be out there, I ended up channeling, through another accident of fate. My sister-in-law came to visit and she said, "I think I'm supposed to be a channel." I said, "OK, I know this lady who does channeling. Maybe she can help."

So we went to see the channel, and I went into a sort of meditative state and floated out of my body. In that state I saw that 'someone' was looking at me. I didn't want to upstage my sister-in-law since this was her night, so I told him to go away. Afterwards I talked to the channeler and I asked her what she thought it meant. She replied, "Well it looks like someone wants to channel through you." I had never thought that I would channel, but I began to look into what channeling was like and ended up channeling as a result.

I had been channeling for about two years when a man invited me to New York to do some channeling. He asked if I could do a guided massage to help his massage therapist in her work with him. I said, "OK, sure, as long as I don't have to open my eyes or touch your body and I get paid." He agreed, "Sure, as long as you tell my massage therapist what to do." I did the session, and when I left my guides told me, in no uncertain terms, that this was the class I needed to teach. That became the starting point for "Access Bars" which are these 32 points on the head that are called the bars. They essentially just delete files on your computer bank so you can have greater clarity, greater ease, greater peace with your body, and more fun.

At the beginning, I did the classes from the child's point of view, and then one day the guides said, "We're done – goodbye." So, since then I've had to develop it. They gave me the basic tools, which were asking questions, never coming to conclusions, and always looking for a different possibility. Those were the primary things that I was given during the channeling thing. And also to learn to trust my own awareness: not to trust anyone else's. That was a very interesting experience and what led me to do what I do today.

My Insight

What insight did you have as a result and how did that affect what you do now?

Part of the insight I got when I was channeling for a woman who was a very spiritual person. Her boyfriend was a Masai prince who had come to the United States and was driving a cab. He had asked her to go back with him and become his first wife. She wasn't sure she could adjust to the culture. She came to me as a client to find out if he was some kind of dark spirit or something. It was very interesting, because in channeling I would always see the light of the being rather than the silliness of their psychology: that's the best way I can describe it. So, when I did a channeling for this lady, I saw that this guy was an incredible being of white light. He was sweet and kind, and caring and loving, and had no subterfuge in his world at all. And then I saw her in a cloak of many colors, where she had all these different aspects of what she was willing to do or be, which had nothing to do with totally being.

That was a huge revelation to me, to realize that you can look at somebody and see who is willing to be clear about everything they choose and yet have no point of view about it – as opposed to somebody who was always trying to make their point of view more right, or more needful or more needed than somebody else. That realization changed my life because I really had only assumed that people said what they meant, and meant what they said. It was very interesting to find out that this was actually not the way it worked with many people. There are beings out in the world that hold no judgment and don't live with judgment. And everybody else is trying to use their judgment as a source of creation, and it's not a source of creation. It's a source of destruction.

One of the precepts of Access Consciousness is that our target in life is to achieve oneness and consciousness. Oneness and consciousness encompasses everything, embraces everything and judges nothing. It includes everything but judges nothing. It was very interesting to realize how many people don't seem to think that they can live their lives without judging. Once you start to really live your life without judgment, everything begins to change. Everything gets bigger and more than I even thought was possible. And from that place, what's happening for me is that I personally am finding that without living in judgment I have greater choice, greater awareness, and there's more that shows up in life than I ever thought was even possible. And there are more realities than we actually see, because our judgment eliminates our awareness of the other realities that can exist.

My Message

What message would you like to leave with the reader?

I'd like people to know that the one thing that is true is that you can change anything. If you realize that you are an infinite being, with the infinite capacity to perceive, to know, to be, and receive and change everything you want, all you have to do is find out who you are judging and stop that, and create different possibilities. And that's how you go about it. Sometimes it just takes a little work.

Bio

Best-selling author, international speaker and a sought-after facilitator, Gary Douglas is known for his intensity of awareness and his incredible capacity to facilitate people to 'know what they know.' He chooses to embody consciousness in everything that he does, which inspires others to choose to become more conscious as a result.

*Gary pioneered a set of transformational life changing tools and processes known as **Access Consciousness®** over 25 years ago. These leading edge tools have transformed the lives of thousands of people all over the world. His work has spread to 53 countries, with 2,300 trained facilitators worldwide. Simple but so effective, the tools facilitate people of all ages and backgrounds to help remove limitations holding them back from a full life.*

Gary has become an internationally recognized thought leader in transforming lives and creating different choices – willing to empower people to see different possibilities and to recognize what is truly possible for them. Gary is acknowledged worldwide for his unique perspectives on personal transformation that are unlike anything else in the world. He is not aligned with any particular religion or tradition. Through his writing and workshops, he gifts processes and tools that bring within reach the ease, joy and glory of life, and the magic of happiness that expand into more awareness, joy and abundance. His simple yet profound teachings have already facilitated countless people throughout the world to 'know what they know' and to realize what they can choose that they never realized they could choose.

Gary has co-hosted a weekly radio show called Conversations in Consciousness *and appears regularly on Voice America. He has been interviewed by TV shows as well as online and print media worldwide including* Good Morning NZ *(New Zealand), AskMen, News.com.au, Daily Edition, Qantas Radio (Australia), Gaiam TV and Playboy Radio (USA). The author of the bestselling novel* **The Place***, this book is about people knowing that all things are possible and choice is the source of creation. Gary is also the coauthor of a variety of books on the subjects of money, relationships, magic and animals with internationally renowned Energy Transformation virtuoso Dr. Dain Heer.*

Gary's website: www.garymdouglas.com

Geoffrey Hoppe

My Tale

Was there a particular event or experience that was a turning point in your life and somehow changed your view of the nature of reality?

It's difficult to narrow it down to just one thing. I really had no spiritual background of any kind, and I think like most people there was kind of a build-up or a stream of things that happened along the way.

It started when I learned hypnosis in high school for a speech project. I had played around with it and hypnotized lots of family and friends. Later when I was in the Army working for NASA, I hypnotized a friend to quit smoking, and he went into a very, very deep trance state. I made the usual suggestions to quit smoking and figured that while he was in a trance I would experiment with something that I had heard about called regression. I took him back to when he was 10 years old, then five years old, and he had extremely vivid recall of very specific incidents. I got him back to when he was about one year old and he was recalling events that I found kind of amazing, because usually we don't have a conscious memory of things until we are about two or three years old. I wondered if he could remember anything from before he was born, so I asked. Quite to my surprise he started recalling past life incidents, one after the other, in detail. He was even living through it emotionally: his body was shaking, and sometimes he had tears, and this was all totally amazing to me because I wasn't even familiar with past lives.

I was so fascinated that I hypnotized him every day for the next week, and we encountered something in the order of 25 or 30 different past lives. This motivated me to start reading books by Edgar Cayce, and the Seth Material by Jane Roberts, but there wasn't much written about past life experiences at that time. I started meditating every day for the next two years, and I found myself wanting to be alone a lot.

I got out of the Army in 1976 and went into the business world. I stopped meditating, stopped reading, totally forgot about the hypnosis and past life stuff. In the 1990s I started to feel this deep longing within me: almost like a constant knocking at the door. Then on April 2, 1995 – I'll never forget that date – I was rifling through a box of books we had been given to find something to read and pulled out a book called *The End Times*, by Lee Carroll. That night after reading sixty-two pages, I put the book down, turned off the lights, and suddenly I felt the presence of two angels next to me. They said, "We're going to take you on a journey." And they did.

It was a journey into incredible celestial realms – almost indescribable – that lasted for about two hours. I was aware that I was lying in bed, I was aware of my body and that it was getting very warm, yet it was unlike anything I had ever known before. I remember saying to myself that I have to remember every detail, because it was so phenomenal, but as I reentered 'normal' reality I could feel it burning away, like the space shuttle on reentry. I was forgetting the details but not the essence.

It was now about 2 am, and since I was wide awake and overwhelmed, I went outside and sat underneath the big oak tree in our yard. A big wind came up. It was a still, spring night but this wind whirled all around the tree. There was no wind among any of the other trees. It was just where I was, and I knew in that moment that my life was never going to be the same.

Not long after that I was flying home from a business trip and found myself nodding off. Suddenly I heard a very clear voice outside of me that announced itself, saying, "I am Tobias. I am here to work with you." I quickly opened my eyes thinking somebody was talking to me, but there was no one anywhere near me. I closed my eyes and again clearly heard the same voice saying, "I am Tobias. I'm here to work with you." Then he continued talking to me for about an hour. I don't remember the details of the conversation, I just remember feeling great affection for this being. I figured he was an angel, or something like that. It was an amazing experience, and much more clear than my previous two experiences. The next day I was getting ready for work and I actually got kind of depressed and angry. It had been a lovely experience, but I wondered if I was just making it up, if I was just working too hard. I thought maybe I was going crazy, so I was getting very angry and saying to myself, "You just need to focus on work. You've got a lot going on so forget about all this other stuff and stop playing this game with yourself."

Exactly one week later I was driving home from work – I have an hour drive each way – and Tobias came in again. When he started talking I was actually delighted he was back, but still confused about whether or not the experience was 'real.'

After that, Tobias came in every single day on my way home from work, like clockwork, and would talk to me. During that first year he basically took me through spiritual boot camp. I didn't know a lot about anything spiritual other than Edgar Cayce and some of the Seth Material, which I never really understood. So this spiritual boot camp was teaching me how to feel – not from an emotional standpoint but through sensory perception – how to feel energies in people and even inanimate objects, like a stop sign. I learned to feel into all the different layers of matter – feeling into the core materials that went into objects; feeling into all the people who would ever see the stop sign. It was really a very wonderful moment when I understood what Tobias was trying to do with me. During this year I hadn't told anybody about my buddy Tobias. I just figured he was a spirit guide or something like that.

I finally realized that I needed to tell my wife Linda, because I was going through so many changes. She was so relieved that there wasn't another woman in my life, but only an old dead Jew, that she took it in stride. Linda said she'd like to talk to Tobias, so I tried to contact him, and that was the first channel session I'd ever done.

When I started talking to Tobias I didn't really have any expectations. I thought he was just a spirit guide, but he was giving me such enormous insight about the other realities and of the true nature of this reality. The definitive shift came in 2001. I had just come back to my aviation job after a weekend conference I gave with Lee Carroll. I was just not in the mood to get back into that corporate stuff and my boss called me into the office and said, "I'd like you to work from home from now on." I was being terminated, which was a minor blow to the ego and especially since I was one of the co-founders of the company, but I would never have quit on my own.

I took some time off and then the phones started ringing. We began getting invitations from around the world to do workshops, which we hadn't even considered before. My first overseas workshop was in England on 9/11 2001. We felt the world really shift at that time, and that somehow my personal experiences with Tobias all tied in.

My Insight
What insight did you have as a result and how did that affect what you do now?

I learned along the way that this thing we call awakening, or enlightenment, is actually a very natural process. We can resist it, we can think about it, worry about it, but we already allowed it for ourselves at some level. This is a time of integrating the divine into the human, while we are still embodied in this planet. Any awakening, whether it's personal or global, causes tremendous upheaval because we're going from an old system to a new one, and our bodies are changing at the DNA level – and even deeper than that. We're also learning to go beyond the mind as our only tool, and starting to bring in things like sensory awareness, what some people call divine intelligence or intuition, or what we call gnosis or true inner knowing. If we just allow it, it's an amazing process.

My Message

What message would you like to leave with the reader?

You're not alone, and you're not crazy! There's a tendency to think you're going crazy when awakening, and you do go through periods of elation and depression. I would highly recommend, particularly when you're going through periods of anxiety or depression, not to take the antidepressant medicines that are handed out like candy by doctors who unfortunately don't understand the awakening process. These medications will completely inhibit your awakening process – something that is very natural and exciting.

There are millions of people around the world waking up, and you can connect with them through Lee Carroll's work, Steve Rother's work, Gregg Braden, or the Crimson Circle. There are many gathering places for those who are awakening, places free from dogma. I would say that awakening is coming into conscious awareness. As human beings we generally have pretty limited focus – getting through life lessons, learning about love, and just trying to make ends meet. Awakening will truly change how you view things and operate within this reality. It is a process of becoming much more aware of why you are here and of yourself as a divine creator being – the 'I Am.'

The masters of the past, like Buddha or Yeshua, had their awakening and then pretty quickly ascended and left the physical realm. For the new era masters, however, it's about mastering the ability to allow the divinity in your life. In other words, to stay here on this planet, because humanity really needs to see humans who are in their divine light, and not distant Masters who are hard to relate to. Ascension is not about suddenly getting it and blasting off; it's about being an awakened, conscious, embodied divine being in this reality. And the real masters will find grace, which is about giving up the struggle and finally allowing all energies to serve you, and then suddenly everything in your life, just... is... there.

Bio

Geoffrey Hoppe founded the Crimson Circle (www.crimsoncircle.com) in 1999 and has guided it to what it has now become: a global affiliation of New Energy teachers with the purpose of inspiring consciousness. The Crimson Circle has grown into a worldwide organization with monthly live webcasts, over 400 certified teachers and a large website presence with 23 foreign language translations. He is also the co-founder of the Awakening Zone international radio network for empowered awakening (www.awakeningzone.com) with over 50 shows per month around the world. Geoffrey has authored three books including **Masters in the New Energy** *and* **Live Your Divinity***. He and his wife Linda travel over 100,000 miles each year presenting the spiritual messages of Adamus Saint-Germain.*

Geoffrey's website: www.crimsoncircle.com

Georgina Cannon

My Tale

Was there a particular event or experience that was a turning point in your life and somehow changed your view of the nature of reality?

I was born in England, and growing up we always knew that there were fairies at the bottom of the garden, and we knew about ghosts and about things paranormal. These were taken for granted; it wasn't a big deal. It was only when I came to North America that I realized what a big deal it was. By the way, I have always seen auras and didn't realize what they were.

While I was a journalist in England I had to shut all that down because it got in the way. When I came to Canada, I realized that not many people really regarded such phenomena as normal. After working as a journalist I opened my own Public Relations company, which was bought by a very large PR company, and suddenly I became corporate. I ended up being one of two senior women in this worldwide company. And although it was glamorous and wonderful in many, many ways, including an expansive expense account and flying everywhere in the world to work with clients and boards of directors, I always felt like I was living a false life, because corporate values were not my values. I ended up running the company in Canada, and we were the only branch offices that wouldn't take certain clients. For example, I would not take on the tobacco industry, the fur industry, or the paper industry, because it went against my ethics. For a large international PR company, taking such a position was quite shocking. My peers would say, "And then there's Georgina with her whacky ideas." But I always made the bottom line, even though we hadn't taken on these accounts.

I really had an '*aha*' moment one morning. One of our prime ministers, Pierre Elliott Trudeau, used to walk in the snow to make his decisions. I went on a mountain retreat. I went on a climb in the mountains in the Adirondacks, needing to feel the power in the majesty of nature – the eagles flying overhead, the wildflowers living under conditions that would seem impossible for anything to flourish – and I came down from the mountain knowing that these golden handcuffs were not worth it and I couldn't continue. I left the corporate world and knew that I was going to downsize, because I was going to do something that was good for the soul. I wasn't sure what it was at that time, but I knew that I had to be true to myself. My daughter was very upset because she liked her mom being a mogul, and she stroked my arm and said, "I know you want to spread your wings, but don't lose any feathers." So I took a year off and literally watched squirrels play and flowers grow.

My Insight

What insight did you have as a result and how did that affect what you do now?

I had already taken some classes in color therapy, aromatherapy, and Gestalt psychology and got my Reiki Master Certification. I did all that because I was interested in it, and then I happened upon hypnosis. It was really a huge learning, because I realized that through the subconscious we can connect with the superconscious, and we can change the blueprint. It wouldn't be me doing any healing; I would be enabling the client to do it. So I took that course, this is now 18 years ago, and within six months I was busy every day with clients, I opened a school, which grew into Canada's largest hypnosis school and clinic. Three years ago I passed it on to someone else and now I am just seeing clients three days a week, teaching part time at the University of Toronto and privately, and writing books.

One of the reasons I decided to sell this thriving business six or seven years ago is that I woke up one morning with a very clear voice in my ear saying, "It's time to teach where you're not." I'm not clairvoyant, I'm clairaudient: that's how I get my messages and connect with guides. And I thought, well that's charming, what does that mean? So I mulled it over. I was already having TV interviews and had done some past life regression programs for the CBC, so I realized it meant to use my journalism, use my writing ability, and start teaching and seeing clients through the Internet – or any other way that allowed me not to be there in person. So I started writing more books, and I started thinking about different ways to reach out. I had made a couple of DVDs on helping people help themselves.

I have this wisdom that is downloaded. It's not mine, and I make this very clear in most of the books I write. Once I've finished writing a book, I usually then sit down and read it through – and I'm surprised by some of the information in it – it's 70% downloaded. "Teach where you're not" opened my life to unfold in amazing ways.

I also received a lovely confirmation about my guides. I was teaching a course on life between lives, and one of the protocols that students had to do was to practice on each other and report. I was demonstrating it and one of the chaps working for me at that time was my subject for demonstration. At one point I said, "Ask your guide his or her name." And he said, "You know it." And I said, "No I don't." Well, sometimes guides play games – they have a sense of humor. So I said that no I don't know, but if you prefer not to tell, that's fine. And he said, "You know it. You know who it is, because I have your guide." And I said, "Oh really, and what's my guide's name?" And he said the name. The hair on the back of my neck stood up, because there's no way that he would have known the name of my guide since I don't tell anybody. I was so surprised, and then we all laughed. There's no way he could have known.

So that was a big 'aha' moment, my reconfirmation of working with my guides, and sometimes I do work with an archangel as well. I've learned not to be casual or flippant about my interaction with them. For example, I wouldn't say, "Oh, should I really sit down and write today?" I know, it's not a circus, and they're not there to perform for us but sometimes it doesn't hurt to just have some fun with them. I tell my clients that when you connect with your guides do so with honor and respect and humility.

Sometimes when I'm working with a client and I can't find my way through, I hear very clearly, "Here's a pathway," and I follow it. It's very honoring work and it's extraordinary and humbling to be the witness to it.

When I first started hearing voices I thought it was a bit strange, and I looked around to see where they came from. But it wasn't the cat talking, or the dog, so I said to myself, "Okay, I'm fine with it being me." I don't know why I wasn't surprised. I expected to see things because I see energy, but clairaudience doesn't come in that way. So when I started having the conversation I realized that's just the way it is. Honestly, not much surprises me, and not much has ever surprised me: the only thing that truly shocks me is unkindness and cruelty.

My Message
Is there a message you would like to leave with the reader?

Yes, yes! You are so much more than you seem. We are all magnificent creatures. Find a way to uncover and discover your magnificence, and honor it, respect it and live it!

Bio

Georgina is an award-winning teacher, author, change catalyst, corporate speaker, international facilitator, and board-certified, master consulting hypnotist. In 1997 she founded the Ontario Hypnosis Centre, which within a few years became Canada's leading hypnosis training facility and clinic. She has since sold the OHC to focus on her writing, lecturing and client work. An accredited life coach, she is recognized as the public face of hypnosis and the mind-body connection in Canada and is a respected member of the complementary health community. Georgina is a regular guest on national and international television and radio programs, and her work has gained her prominence as a source for news and feature articles on hypnosis, relationship counseling, and complementary therapies. Georgina's third and most recent book is **Return Again: How to Find Meaning in Your Past Lives and Your Interlives.**

Georgina's website: georginacannon.com

Gregg Braden

My Tale

Was there a particular event or experience that was a turning point in your life and somehow changed your view of the nature of reality?

I was trained in the sciences and worked as a geologist with Phillips Petroleum during the energy crisis, and later with Martin Marietta, also in crisis management. It was a very frightening time, the last years of the Cold War when the superpowers came unthinkingly close to unleashing the power of nuclear weapons on civilian populations.

I took some time off and went to the Sinai Peninsula in Egypt, where I had an unusual experience. I climbed Mount Sinai in the wee hours of the morning and got to the top at sunrise. I have always been powerfully moved by natural beauty. It's been one of the prime motivators in my life. Looking out over the astounding beauty of the sunrise over the Sinai desert that morning I felt something open inside me. I asked myself this question in my mind: "If I died in this moment, if I left the world at this moment and could never come back, and looked at everything that I'd accomplished until now in my life, would I feel complete with my time in this world?" And before I could even complete the question my body was responding. I felt this heat and something inside of me welling up and screaming, "No!" And the next question was, "What would it take to be able to say yes? What would it take for me to say that I feel complete with the gift of my life in this world?" That experience became my compass, my reference point.

I left Cairo to return to the US on a 5:30 am flight one morning shortly after that, and the next morning I was at my desk at Martin Marietta writing software for nuclear weapons. I took an early lunch and sat and stared out the window, feeling such a disconnect between my work and my experience in the Sinai.

And I asked myself another question.

Now, you know I was trained as a scientist, and I had been taught that the scientific method was a way to solve problems. Science has always said that you have to choose between spirituality or religion and science, but you cannot have both. I realized I had to make a choice. But I didn't agree with that because there are 5,000 years of spiritual traditions that came before science. They weren't very scientific, but they had very good answers. They told us in their own way where human life comes from, what is our relationship to ourselves, what is our relationship to other people, what is our relationship to the past, how do we go about solving our problems. And when I looked closely, science couldn't really answer some of those questions.

So in that moment I asked myself the next question: "What would happen if we married these two great ways of knowing into a wisdom that is greater than either could be alone?" Spirituality obviously does not have all the answers and is not meeting the needs for the crises and the extremes that we're having in the world today, and science doesn't have all the answers either. What if we take the nuts and bolts of the science that tell us truthfully, honestly, factually how things work – that's knowledge – and then we use the wisdom of 5,000 years of human experience to apply that knowledge in our lives and in our world? Where would that lead? And my answer to that question has been the next point on my compass; it is the yardstick by which I gauge every choice that I make or every decision about the opportunities that cross my path almost every day – and they're all good ones.

I get amazing invitations and opportunities for film projects, books, foundations, to be on the board of some amazing organizations, or to be at the startup of corporations that are hoping to fulfill spiritual needs in a scientific way. This yardstick is what helps me choose, what gets me closer to being able to say yes to that original question, "Would I feel complete if I left the world today?"

And, I will always do the very best I can do. In doing that, I fulfill my commitment and free myself from the magnet that holds me here, and find the things that make my heart sing. I've applied this at so many times and in so many circumstances, and that's why I'm sharing this here.

My Insight
What insight did you have as a result and how did that affect what you do now?

What I made a choice to do was to simply use science to tell us factually what our relationship is to ourselves and the world. As a scientist, what I discovered early on is that there is a chain of knowledge that links our modern world with the past. And that chain has been broken many times over the centuries – for example, the burning of the library at Alexandria in 4th century BC. Over 53,000 scrolls were destroyed at that time, many of them already ancient scrolls of healing and medicine. There were Egyptian scrolls talking about optics and how to use energy in people's homes. Those were destroyed in the 4th century AD when 45 books were removed from the modern biblical canon. The ones that were left were incomplete because we found different texts in the edited Dead Sea Scrolls, in the Nag Hammadi library. Many biblical scholars will openly and honestly admit that the Bible has been revised significantly from its original text. And the reason this is important is that when you look at the original texts they answer some of the deepest mysteries, and the biggest questions about healing and life. So, I've spent almost 30 years going to the source, exploring some of the most remote, isolated, pristine and beautiful places remaining on the earth that have preserved the wisdom of the past. And my job, as I've defined it, is to take this wisdom and marry it with the best science of today to give us real answers and real solutions that apply in the real world.

I just completed a tour in Europe, and everywhere I went people would ask if I was going to talk about spiritual stuff, or all the other stuff. And I always reply to this question with another question: "Where do you draw the line?" You draw me the line that separates spirituality from everyday stuff, and the minute you do that, you fall into the ancient trap that separates us from the truth and from the ability to apply that truth in our lives and in the world in a meaningful way. If we are ever going to apply in our lives the things that we claim to be true in our hearts, I cannot think of a better time than right now in the world of extremes where we are being pushed to the limits and boundaries of our very survival; I cannot imagine what could be a more spiritual endeavor than to apply the deepest truths of life in our everyday world. To me, that's where the boundary between science and spirituality dissolves.

My Message
What message would you like to leave with the reader?

One hundred and fifty years of scientific thinking has led us to believe a story of our relationship to ourselves and the world. That story has been one of separation: that we are separate from our bodies, we are separate from the earth, we are separate from our past, and that we solve our problems through competition and conflict. New peer-reviewed science has changed the story. And the new story tells us that we are deeply connected to our bodies, we are deeply connected to this earth and to our past, and that nature is actually based upon a model of cooperation and what biologists call mutual aid – not the competition and the conflict described by Darwin in 1859.

So with that in mind, every choice we make, the way we deal with every crisis, every situation that crosses our path, from relationships and jobs, or careers to health situations, the old science led us to believe that we ask the question, "What can I get from the world that exists, what's in it for me?" That's the belief that we're separate and that competition is the way things work. The new science changes the question. The question now is, *"What can I give to the world that's emerging? What can I share, what can I contribute to the new world that's emerging?"* And I'm going to invite our readers to please not be deceived by the simplicity of the question, because the way we answer that question for us changes everything. It opens the doors of new possibilities of job and career in ways that we had never imagined within the thinking of the separation of the past.

So what I would leave readers with is an invitation to change the question from what can I get from the world that exists to *What can I give, what can I share, what can contribute to the world that's emerging?*

Bio

New York Times best-selling author **Gregg Braden** *is internationally renowned as a pioneer in bridging science, ancient wisdom, and the real world! Following a successful career as a computer geologist for Phillips Petroleum during the 1970s energy crisis, he worked as a Senior Computer Systems Designer with Martin Marietta Defense Systems during the final years of the Cold War. In 1991, he became the first Technical Operations Manager for Cisco Systems.*

For more than 27 years Gregg has explored high mountain villages, remote monasteries, and forgotten texts to merge their timeless secrets with the best science of today. His discoveries are now shared in 33 countries and 38 languages through such paradigm-inspiring books as: **The God Code; The Divine Matrix; Fractal Time; Deep Truth;** *and his newest,* **The Turning Point: Creating Resilience in a Time of Extremes.**

Gregg is an active member of several leadership organizations, including the Evolutionary Leadership think tank, founded by Deepak Chopra in 2008, and has received numerous awards in recognition of his insights and innovation. Gregg's work has been shared on every continent of the world and in recent years he has presented his seminars and trainings to Fortune 500 companies, the United Nations, the US military, international businesses and is now featured in media specials on the History Channel, the Discovery Channel, National Geographic and ABC.

Gregg's website: www.greggbraden.com

Gyorgyi Szabo

My Tale

Was there a particular event or experience that was a turning point in your life and somehow changed your view of the nature of reality?

There were a series of events in my life that actually changed the way I look at the world, and the way I look at myself. I was born in Hungary within a family that is predominantly atheist. Yet as a child I always looked at the sky and wondered what was in the cosmos, asking questions like, *why are we here* and *why am I here?* Years later when I started my studies at university, I yearned to explore what other people said about the nature of the universe, and began reading books on philosophy. But the Western philosophers left so many questions unanswered, so I felt that I must venture on, I must find out more.

I started my Master's degree and I decided this time to focus on Eastern traditions – Buddhism, Taoism, Hinduism. These worldviews really ignited a spark in me. I came across a book called *Science and the Akashic Field*, written by Ervin Laszlo, and a light started shining brightly in my consciousness: I realized that this is it! This is the explanation for 'everything' that I was looking for. It encompassed all my understanding because the Akasha Paradigm in fact denotes a verb – it is *being* and *becoming* at the same time. Our world is not just things moving about in space and time – that's only the surface; below it there is an inter-connected, holographically in-formed, and fundamentally whole world where all things inter-penetrate all other things. As a result, we may say that our universe can be understood as an all-pervasive consciousness that expresses itself in space and time, energy and matter, through geometric patterns at all scales of existence.

When I came to realize the concept of the Akasha Paradigm, I felt it in every single cell of my body. I wanted to know more and to fully experience this interconnection. I immediately delved into the literature of quantum science, cosmology, energy fields, altered states of consciousness and near-death experiences, reincarnation, and so on. Over time I become more aware of 'energy flows and blockages' in my own and in other people's bodies, and signed up for courses to pursue this interest.

Recently I had a profound experience with a therapist friend, which truly changed my life. While in an altered state of consciousness, I was catapulted to a cosmic level: I didn't feel my body anymore. I felt that it was my consciousness that was looking, observing, and actively participating at the same time. I saw stars, planets all around, and our earth below me. I was in this infinite space where there was no fear or anxiety, only calmness and peace, and a sense of an all-pervading consciousness.

In that state, I questioned whether I was the only one present. I saw some interesting 'things' passing by and asked, "Is there a different consciousness beyond what I am experiencing?" There was no response. I thought that perhaps the question was too obvious, or maybe my consciousness is not evolved enough to deserve an answer. Then, I had the thought that I wanted to meet others in this space and time. I heard a question: "Who would you like to meet?" I said, "I would like to meet God." I'm not a religious person, but always have been very spiritual.

Suddenly a tiny white light appeared that escalated in size, and I felt immediately drawn toward it. I wanted to be with it or immersed by it. At that moment, I heard the voice of my therapist friend calling me back, telling me to open my eyes. When I did, I felt like I was in a different world, but I didn't know which world was real – this one or where I had just been. I knew that I wasn't delusional, yet I really wanted to stay in that other dimension, one that seemed infinite, expansive, and filled with love.

My Insight

What insight did you have as a result and how did that affect what you do now?

This experience opened further my ever-expanding horizon. Now I live with less fear and I have a stronger sense of purpose. I feel that I'm on this planet for a reason and I'm still discovering and uncovering that reason. I actually had the experience that I am more than just a three-or four-dimensional being. I experienced the infinity of consciousness, and now I am convinced about the immortality of consciousness.

My Message

What message would you like to leave with the reader?

I know that I am a conscious being and so are all humans. We have freedom to act consciously and to make conscious choices. We experience turbulent events locally and globally, and there are lots of challenges ahead of us. But I do believe that together, collectively, we can create a sustainable world that is respectful of nature and respectful of every single human being on this planet. I feel that I have a wholeness-consciousness whereby I realize that I'm not separate from the world around me – and I know that no one else is separate either. The entire concept of separation is absolutely false: it is an illusory concept.

When we act with that separation in mind we divide the unity of the world and segment its wholeness into bits and pieces. Our ego is what divides us, but our body does not follow suit. It acts in coherence with the whole earth, and I know that I'm part of the earth, part of the larger whole. We live in a wonderfully interconnected universe, and I realize that I am an integral part of that wonderful world. I am a member of the human and earth community, and I try to live my life in a way that respects all of humanity and nature.

This is not a choice for me. I really feel it is my duty, and even more so, it simply is the way I am – a human being empowered with the consciousness of oneness and belonging. Everyone on this planet is the same. This is the message I would like to convey.

Bio

Gyorgyi Szabo was Co-Founder, Vice President, and Academic Dean at the Ervin Laszlo Center for Advanced Study. She served as the Executive Director of the Exploratoria Program at the same Center. She was co-creator of the WorldShift International Foundation, and the WorldShift 2012 organizations, and Advisory Board Member of the Memnosyne Foundation USA. Gyorgyi and Ervin Laszlo co-organized an international event with the Chinese government for "Building an Eco-Civilization," in Hangzhou, China 2013. Since 2013 she became a member of the Executive Committee of the Club of Budapest France. In 2012, Gyorgyi founded, and serves as a president of an association UniverSoul, a Hub for Conscious Evolution Paris, working with Barbara Marx Hubbard. In 2008 she acted as the International Relations Associate for the Club of Budapest Foundation in Hungary and remains a Creative Member of that organization. In 2010 she translated from Italian to English **The Basic Code of the Universe: The Science of the Invisible in Physics, Medicine, and Spirituality** *by Dr. Massimo Citro. She gives lectures worldwide and her articles have been published in the Scientific and Medical Network's Review,* The Network Review; The Shift Network; and World Futures: The Journal of General Evolution. *She is a trained Reiki and Reconnective Healing practitioner.*

Gyorgyi holds a Master's degree from Trinity Saint David, University of Wales, a Bachelor's degree from Birkbeck College, University of London, and is presently researching her dissertation on the scientific theories of Ervin Laszlo for her PhD at the Sorbonne, the University of Paris. She has lived in the USA, the UK, Italy and Spain, and her holistic approach to metaphysics and interest in conscious evolution serves as the foundation to her work in helping to facilitate our shared evolution toward a peaceful, just, and sustainable world.

She lives in Paris, France.

Gyorgyi can be contacted at:
fr.linkedin.com/pub/gyorgyi-szabo/30/403/301

Howard Falco

My Tale

Was there a particular event or experience that was a turning point in your life and somehow changed your view of the nature of reality?

Yes, the turning point was when I didn't know the reason for existence anymore. My whole life I thought I knew the reason for existence – or at least I thought I had the answers, which was you check off things that you're supposed to do, that you're supposed to create in life, that are supposed to make you happy. And what happened was that the more I accumulated, well not the less happy I got, but I didn't achieve that state I thought I would achieve. I had fallen in love and gotten married, I had two wonderful kids, a job I wanted, a home – pretty much everything on my checklist. I thought the last thing that I needed to do was to make millions of dollars. And then one day I realized that money was not going to change even one of the major or important things in my life – it was not to change the relationships, it was not going to change the things that truly mattered. And when I realized that, my last excuse for not being happy and content was gone, I was out of answers.

That was the turning point because at that moment I was staring into the abyss of *I don't know*. And I had a yearning and a desire to know that surpassed any yearning I ever had in my life. That's when I hit my deepest point of desperation, lifted my arms up and just said, "I'm ready to know. I'm ready to know every answer I can possibly be shown." Not being spiritual or religious at the time I asked these questions in my mind or to whatever one's idea of God is, or just out to the universe. That was the turning point – the true opening to the beginning of the incredible answers that were starting to come into my awareness.

My Insight

What insight did you have as a result and how did that affect what you do now?

Two weeks after that moment when I cried out with a deep sense of yearning, I happened to be in a seminar at work, some of which was related to the psychology of the mind in relation to the financial markets. I started seeing the information coming to me in a different way – more as it related to life in general. And in one instant I realized that this idea of happiness, or the control and power over it that I always thought was something outside that needed to be attained, was always truly on the inside. That was a great sense of relief, understanding that the power was within me.

The other thing I realized was that this perfection I was searching for through these outside things was already there in who I was at that very moment, and everything that had led to that very moment. There was a perfection to the process that I was beginning to see. This realization led to another amazing insight, which was that life is like a big answering machine: the more intense your questions, the more life delivers you the answers. And the way that these answers come through is in your regular walk of life. So what you really need to do is just be a little more present to the coincidences that are always around you in the happenings of your life. That got me really excited and I felt like I had opened Pandora's box.

I decided to fire off a whole bunch more questions because I was so excited, knowing that all I had to do was be present. Over the next four months, the answers to all those questions started to come in faster and faster, and peaked in a second experience four months after the first one: time had collapsed between question and answer and all of a sudden I was getting an instantaneous download of everything happening all at once. That was a very, very humbling and powerful moment in my life, which is detailed in the introduction to my book, *I Am.*

That moment, and that insight, changed everything for me. It took me a couple of years to get my arms around the information, because the old voice in my head tried to pull me back to my old self by saying, "Who do you think you are and why do you think anybody's going to believe you, and how does this happen to someone who just has an ordinary life? This sacred insight is not for you, that's for the sages of all time." It took me a couple of years to finally break completely free of that voice and realize that this *did* happen, and this *is* for everybody, and my personal mission in life is to honor the grace I experienced by sharing it for the rest of my life.

My Message

What message would you like to leave with the reader?

That the great power in life is always within you, waiting to be revealed. Waiting for the moment of your readiness to embrace more of your perfection and more of your unlimited value and worth. Then to go out and honor that perfection in your every thought and action, because that's truly what leads to a completely different experience of life. It takes a certain readiness, and everyone has their own free will and timetable to that place. But life will be there to support you at every single step along the way. Even the times that you don't think it's supporting you because there's suffering, know that suffering has a purpose and it's directly related to your deepest questions and requests.

Bio

Howard Falco is a modern-day spiritual teacher, self-empowerment expert and speaker specializing in self-awareness and the power of the mind as it relates to the creation of the experience of life. He is the author of two books on human understanding, creativity and potential, **I AM: The Power of Discovering Who You Really Are** *and* **Time in a Bottle: Mastering the Experience of Life** *(Penguin Group).*

In late 2002, in the middle of ordinary life, this married father of two went through a sudden and extraordinary expansion of mind. The dramatic depth and breadth of this shift in consciousness unveiled the answers to many of the largest and deepest questions that humanity seeks answers for on a regular basis, such as "Who am I?", "Why am I here?", "How do I overcome suffering?", and "How do I achieve lasting peace and fulfillment?" During this enlightenment the core essence underlying all human creation, action, reaction, joys and suffering was revealed to him. Stunned and inspired by this powerful knowledge, Howard set out to honor what happened by sharing what he learned.

For Howard, the most thrilling revelation of his new insight is that everyone has the same opportunity to experience this information and the freedom, joy and creative power it brings. He states, "The issue is not whether the access or answers to any of your questions exist, but only a matter of if you are ready to embrace the new way of looking at and experiencing the world that these answers will bring."

His books empower readers to new possibilities by unveiling the wisdom and the answers regarding how and why each of us have created our unique and individual experience of reality. This is done while simultaneously offering the practical and empowering insight on how to take complete control of the creative process of life from this precious moment forward.

More information about his books, private coaching, and schedule can be found at Howard's websites.

Howard's websites: www.HowardFalco.com
www.ThebookIAM.com

Irene Kendig

My Tale

Was there a particular event or experience that was a turning point in your life and somehow changed your view of the nature of reality?

Yes. It was 2006, and I'd just started a Master's program in spiritual psychology. About that time, a friend called to tell me about Jana, a woman with an extraordinary gift: she could communicate with people on the other side. Jana wanted to make this her life's work, so my friend asked if I'd be willing to schedule a session. I hesitated; I had a lot on my plate. My friend noticed my hesitation and said Jana wouldn't charge anything, she'd just want me to tell others if I thought she was the real deal. I agreed, and scheduled a phone appointment.

It was a Thursday afternoon. I was sitting on the futon in my home office, my dog Scooter on one side of me and a pad of paper and pen on the other. After we exchanged greetings, Jana asked me for the name of someone with whom I wanted to connect.

"Beba," I said. I didn't tell her that Beba was my mother or that she'd passed three years earlier. Jana began to accurately describe my mother, and then asked, "Did Beba like to play cards? Because she's playing cards. She says she's winning; she's laughing!"

My mother practically greeted people at the door with a deck of cards. She loved gin rummy. In fact, some of our most profound conversations took place over games of gin rummy.

"That sounds like Beba," I said.

"She has a daughter?" Jana asked.

"Yes."

"She says her daughter doesn't consider herself a good mother; she says that's nonsense."

My jaw dropped. I was eighteen when I gave birth to my son

David, and still carried guilt about not having been the parent I thought I should have been.

Jana asked if I had any questions for Beba, but the only thing that came out of my mouth was, "So, how *are* you?"

During that session, Jana connected me with three more loved ones on the other side. Each one came through in a way that was irrefutable. At the end of that call, I danced around my house for a couple of hours, rejoicing in the shift in consciousness that had taken place: I knew – without a doubt – that we go on. I knew with certainty that we are eternal.

I called Jana and scheduled a second appointment for the following week. At the end of that session, I asked her if she wanted to collaborate on a book. She said yes. We agreed to work by phone for an hour a day, five days a week. We did this for two years.

The dialogues became *Conversations with Jerry and Other People I Thought Were Dead*, which went on to win seven national awards. In it, I speak with seven loved ones, asking each the same question: "What did you experience when you released your last breath on earth?" Hearing what they had to say transformed the way I live my life.

My Insight

What insight did you have as a result and how did that affect what you do now?

It changed my life in several ways. All seven people, for example, concurred on a life review that takes place in a space of unconditional love. We review every moment of our earthly existence without judgment – but not just from *our* perspective. We see ourselves from the perspective of others – people, animals, plants, and all sentient life. So, when I review my life, I'll see myself from the perspective of the people I affected.

I distinctly remember the day this information came through. That afternoon, as I was standing in line at the grocery store, I realized that I was affecting the people around me simply by the thoughts I was thinking, which influenced my attitude and vibration. When I became consciously aware of the impact I was having, I became more mindful, respectful and responsible for my energy at any given moment. If I'm going to relive each moment from the perspective of life around me, I want to make sure that each moment – to the best of my ability – is a good one.

Another insight came from Jared, one of my loved ones on the other side who transitioned when he was thirty.

"Is there anything you miss about being on earth?" I asked him.

"No, there really isn't anything; I have everything I want and need. But I *would* like for my family to know that I'm alive. *I* know, but they don't… and it makes them sad. Loneliness is my family falsely believing that they don't have any place to put their love for me."

As a Soul-Centered Life Coach, I work with people facing all kinds of challenges, from eliminating regret and remorse to clarifying and manifesting their life purpose. I encourage grieving clients to talk with their loved ones as if their transitioned loved ones could hear them. I invite them to explore ways to honor their loved ones by expressing the love that still exists. After all, it's the love that connects us – and continues to connect us – even though a person has transitioned and is no longer in physical form. The relationship changes, but it doesn't end. We have to find new ways to relate to our transitioned loved ones.

Throughout my life, I've had some interesting death-related experiences. Let me tell you one such story.

It was 1976. I was a single mother living with my six-year-old son, David, in a North Hollywood duplex. It was a sweet two-bedroom/one bath with a fenced-in patio. I loved that duplex. With no one above us, and no one below us, it was as close to living in a house as the two of us had come since I'd divorced David's dad five years prior. I heard a knock at my front door.

When I opened it, my brother Joe was standing there, holding a cardboard box with a crow sitting on top.

"I caught my neighbor's kid shooting a BB gun at a bird's nest above their garage. A crow fell out of the nest and onto the driveway. A cat was ready to pounce on it. I rescued it and took it to the vet. It's got two broken legs. Would you like to take care of it?"

I stared, wide-eyed, at the big black crow sitting atop a cloth that stretched from one end of the box to the other. A closer look revealed casts on the crow's legs, dangling through two holes that had been cut in the center of the cloth.

"Would you like to take care of it?" my brother repeated.

"I... I would be honored," I responded.

Honored? That's a strange response. Where did that come from? Perhaps my heart and soul recognized what my mind didn't yet know, that this was a blessing of extraordinary measure.

I immediately called the vet.

"Hi. My name is Irene, and I'm taking care of the crow with the broken legs – but, I don't know how to be with the crow. Can you tell me how to *be* with the crow?"

"Oh, just be yourself," the vet answered.

I named the crow Marty, and we slowly got to know each other over the next few days. Sometimes Marty would let me stroke his head, and sometimes he would snap at me as if to say, "I'm in pain. Leave me alone." I learned to take my cues from Marty.

One Sunday morning, a couple of weeks into the experience, I awoke with a sense that Marty had crossed over during the night. I breathed a sigh of relief when I walked into the dining room and found him sitting atop his box, very much alive. It was a spectacular day, so I carried Marty out to the patio and carefully placed him – still in his box – on the patio floor to bask in the warm sunshine.

I strolled inside, located the Barbra Streisand *Classical* album, put the record on the stereo, and sat down, nude, in the doorway leading out to the patio. I closed my eyes. The sun gently warmed my 20-something body as Barbra's devotional hymns to God caressed my soul. When the music finished, I opened my eyes and looked over at Marty. He had peacefully crossed over.

My son David and I said a prayer and buried Marty in our yard.

Later that day, I went over to my friend Karen's house. I hadn't seen her or spoken with her in a few weeks, so she knew nothing of Marty.

"I'm so glad you're here," she said. "I have a gift for you." She walked into her bedroom and returned with a square 10" x 10" package. I removed the wrapping paper and gasped. I was holding a framed picture of a crow with a rainbow at its back, looking up to the heavens.

My Message
What message you would like to leave with the reader?

There is no wrong way to do life. There is no wrong way to do life! Celebrate! Enjoy! At our essence we are joy. And the more we're able to remove what stands in the way of our experiencing that joy, the more we'll create heaven on earth here and now.

Bio
Irene Kendig is an accomplished speaker, workshop facilitator, soul-centered coach, and international award-winning author. Her first book, **Conversations with Jerry and Other People I Thought Were Dead: Seven compelling dialogues that will transform the way you think about dying… and living***, has been honored with seven national awards and is endorsed by* NY Times *Bestselling Authors, Neale Donald Walsch and Bernie Siegel, MD. She is a trained NLP Practitioner and certified Alchemical Hypnotherapist, with a BA cum laude in Psychology from UCLA and an MA in Spiritual Psychology from the University of Santa Monica (USM).*

Ms. Kendig served as senior corporate trainer for an international management consulting firm that specialized in delivering customer satisfaction, team-building, and problem-solving programs to a vast array of companies. Irene has delivered trainings to AAA, Avis, American Express, Lufthansa, Marriott, Oracle, Sun Microsystems, TeleCheck, Trane, and Tumi – with satisfaction ratings consistently over 95 percent. A gifted public speaker, Ms. Kendig has also taught presentation skills to managers in Corporate America.

Irene is dedicated to living and sharing the ideas, concepts, and soul-centered skills at the heart of spiritual psychology. She serves as simultaneous interpreter (English/Spanish) on a team of 70 USM graduate volunteers who have been bringing these principles and experiential practices to inmates at one of the largest maximum security women's prisons in the world, Valley State Prison for Women (VSPW). The program, "Freedom to Choose," has been nominated for a national award that recognizes excellence in prison reform programs. A moving 22-minute film documents the power of this work, and was a recent winner in the Emerging Filmmaker Showcase at the 2009 Cannes Film Festival.

Ms. Kendig lives in Charlottesville with her husband Charles and their dog Scooter. She is the proud mother of three adult sons, David, Eli, and Josh.

Irene's website: www.irenekendig.com

Jack Rourke

My Tale

Was there a particular event or experience that was a turning point in your life and somehow changed your view of the nature of reality?

I feel that moment-by-moment we have an opportunity to alter our perception of reality by letting go. When we no longer over-identify with our emotional impulses and rationalizations we are free to feel who we really are. Sometimes this is unpleasant. But experiencing discomfort allows us to move through those things that keep us from realizing our inner divinity. For me there was a very interesting experience that occurred when I was a teenager that showed me in a visceral way what it meant to really feel. It also taught me what we perceive as objective reality might not be real at all.

Let me explain. When I was a teenager my twin sister died. At the moment of her death I had what is called an empathetic near-death experience. It occurred one morning after I finished delivering the newspapers on my Sunday morning route around my neighborhood.

The day my sister died was unusual because normally I was always running behind on my paper route. But on that Sunday, I finished my deliveries early. I came home and made my bed, showered, and ate. I'm not sure how it happened but I actually had so much extra time I decided to lay down. This had never happened in the history of my newspaper career. Since I was wearing church clothes and my bed was already made though, I had to place myself gingerly on top of the bed so as not to mess it up or my clothes. Before long, I drifted off to what I assumed was a short nap.

Not long after lying down I felt a tingling through my body. Then I became aware of a presence. In the open space to the left of my bed above the floor, it was as if a window opened up – or at least this is how my mind conceived of it. From this window I perceived a presence. As I wakened within my mind I felt compelled to sit up and see what was going on. As I sat up, I had an instinct to pull my legs toward me but my legs didn't move. Somehow I was still able to sit up, albeit it in an unnatural way. A second later I realized I was sitting with only my bottom still in my body. I was, essentially, sitting up half in my body and half out. The next thing I remember is that presence reaching its hand out to me. It lifted me from my body and said, "Don't be afraid." Oddly enough I wasn't. I felt nothing, actually. 'He' then repeated himself, saying, "Don't be afraid, your sister is dead."

I didn't have an emotional response at all. I was maybe a bit bewildered, yet it all seemed like a perfectly natural occurrence. Then the being said, "Look," and gestured toward the other side of the bed. I turned my awareness in that direction and there was my sister, standing there. She was smiling at me.

Now, my twin sister had never walked: she spent her entire life in a wheelchair. This is not to say she was terminally ill. Her death was a total shock. But the moment I saw my sister standing there outside her body, I felt a connection between us like never before. When she smiled, the essence of my inner being lit up. I could feel her liberation, I could feel her joy. I could feel who and what she truly was. And in that moment I believe I felt who and what we all truly are.

As I empathetically and seemingly objectively observed my sister's transition into the afterlife, or whatever, I was overwhelmed. I felt like a light bulb being lit by a million watts. I couldn't contain the energy I was feeling. I was overwhelmed with what I can only surmise was pure joy. I honestly can't put into words what this experience felt like. The emotion was so strong it brought tears to my eyes. And it was the sensation of a tear rolling down my cheek that brought my awareness back to my body.

Lying on my bed in the aftermath of this incredible

experience, I tried to go back. I wanted so badly to relive what had just happened. But it was over. The magic of that moment was gone forever and, like my sister, there was no bringing it back.

I lay perfectly still for what felt like hours. A short time later a sibling burst into my room introducing panic into the stillness I had been basking in. It was then that I was told my twin had in fact died.

I never mourned my sister in a conventional way. I only felt excitement and joy. To those not privy to what transpired between my sister and me, her death probably seemed to inspire inexplicable happiness. When I finally left my bedroom and went to the living room where the neighbors and the family pastor were gathered and lamenting my sister's loss, everyone got a shock. As soon as I walked into the room everyone stopped whatever they were doing and just looked at me. The tears suddenly dried, the sobs, the platitudes – everything and everyone froze as if time stood still. My state of being was so completely out of synch with their collective experience it was palpable. I was like a child walking into the living room on Christmas morning, glowing with joyful anticipation and wonder. It really was as if I had been lit from the inside out. No one knew how to react.

My Insight

What insight did you have as a result and how did that affect what you do now?

Since the day of my sister's passing it became clear to me that what we see with our eyes is very different than what reality may be. It's wonderful how during times of crisis one can become very present and alert. Tragedy brings with it an opportunity for a connection between people that otherwise might not be realized. I don't think the folks around me felt this way though, and I certainly didn't identify with the grief or the rituals that occurred after the loss of my sister.

Over the months following her death I was increasingly alienated. I'd overhear adults say cruel things about me as if this was a way to comfort my family. People said things like, "How's the tough guy?" No one actually tried to see me. No one ever asked how I felt. It was much easier for them to deal with their own discomfort with death by not engaging me or anyone else in my family in a meaningful way. It seemed everyone just assumed something was wrong with me since I was so at peace and uplifted. The juxtaposition between my gratitude and joy for an end to my handicapped sister's suffering, magnified by witnessing what seemed to be life after death, and the insensitivity directed at me, taught me to feel ashamed. What I was emanating was so inconsistent emotionally with everyone else that ironically, after feeling so intimately connected with what seemed to be a heavenly experience, I felt abandoned as well. This was my perspective. As a result, I had no one with whom I felt safe sharing the incredible experience I had lived with my departed twin.

A few months later, around our birthday, I was home alone one afternoon. It was raining and I was sitting in a chair looking out our front window feeling sad. I began to question the reality of what happened the day my sister died. I was completely lost in thought, until suddenly the clouds separated. Because everything was still damp, the sun created a beautiful, surreal glow. I closed my eyes and said a short prayer. *"God, if this is all real you have to let me know if my sister's okay."*

My mother had created a shrine to my sister in the living room, across from where I was sitting. My twin used to collect these horrible 19th century-looking porcelain dolls – bulgy-eyed, pasty-faced creatures in old-fashioned garb. Breaking the silence of that contemplative moment, I suddenly heard the chiming of a creepy lullaby, like something out of a slasher movie. I looked at the dolls and one of them was chiming and spinning in a circle.

Every time it turned, its eyes seemed to lock right on me. A chill ran down my spine. *Okay, I get it. Thank you for the sign.* And the instant I said thank you the doll stopped turning and fell quiet.

One could argue the doll spinning could have been the result of some kind of unconscious psychokinetic activity where my mind interfaced with the environment in such a way as to discharge the emotional build-up inside my pubescent body. For me, it was enough to assume there is an intersection between our nonphysical selves and the physical world. One that suggests something beyond what we ordinarily accept as real supports us when we're in need.

I point to the day of my sister's passing as an example of the first time I perceived verifiable information in an extrasensory manner. After all, I perceived my sister outside of her body and was foretold of her death, and when I retuned to ordinary awareness she was, in fact, dead. That single extrasensory perception was a watershed moment for me. I realized there was something else, something more than what we can see.

It was a good 10 years before I really started investigating the nature of my own extrasensory experiences. It was that inquiry which put me on the path to doing what I now do for a living.

Saying that my work has evolved over the years is an under-statement. One of the things I teach my students though – and the thrust of my book *The Rational Psychic*™ – is that the ability to perceive extrasensory information in any form is not the same as being a spiritually developed person. Often the terms psychic and spiritual development are used interchangeably. This is a mistake. There are characteristics that are similar between these two processes, yes. And, one can sometimes lead to the other – but at the end of the day, for the serious spiritual aspirant and the serious psychic student, these two methods of personal devel-opment are decidedly different. As such they should be approached individually with great care and attention to one's emotional life.

My Message

What message you would like to leave with the reader?

Psychic development will impede your spiritual development unless you have the capacity to remain fully embodied, while fully feeling and processing your emotions. This truth is oversimplified here but the importance of this statement cannot be overstressed.

The most significant relationship you can have is with the divine presence within you. To live authentically aligned with this, your fundamental spiritual essence, you can neither stifle nor exaggerate your emotions in paranormal ways. Living your spiritual essence is best realized through compassionate and kind companionship.

Living a spiritual life is never an affect of psychic activity. Walking a spiritual path has nothing to do with nurturing a connection to spirit guides, angels, dead relatives, or any kind of ESP.

Being spiritual means facing reality as it presents itself, while living and knowing confidently that you, as you are, are enough.

When you love yourself enough to allow yourself to be seen in such a way that permits others to be as they are as well, the divine presence that is you manifests as your human being.

Bio

Celebrity Clairvoyant Jack Rourke is the author of the best-selling book, **The Rational Psychic™: A Skeptic's Guide to Extraordinary Perception**, *and one of the most prominent working psychics in North America today.*

Dubbed "world-renowned" by AOL's celebrity news website Pop-Eater.dot.com, Mr. Rourke has been featured on ABC, NBC, FOX, Showtime, the BBC, The History- and Travel Channels, Destination America, and more.

Jack earned the title world-renowned because of his work on criminal and missing person's cases, the fact his predictions and commentary have been distributed globally by CNN and the Associated Press, and because his client base extends well beyond the continental United States. He's also consulted on major Hollywood films. And in 2009, Jack was featured as the real life "Patrick Jane" in a special documentary included within the first season DVD release of the hit TV show The Mentalist. *In this short film Jack discusses psychic police work alongside former FBI and other experts.*

Jack's radio appearances include, but are not limited to, the internationally syndicated Coast to Coast *with George Noory, CBS'* Overnight America *with* Jon Grayson, *the nationally syndicated* Mancow Morning *radio network, Playboy radio, and more.*

Jack's website: www.jackrourke.net

Jake Ducey

My Tale

Was there a particular event or experience that was a turning point in your life and somehow changed your understanding of the nature of reality?

I think that it's ongoing. I think that what I believe varies from day-to-day, but probably what took me off society's prescribed lifestyle path was a comment from my teacher in my freshman year of college. He told me that I couldn't ask questions pertaining to current events because those things weren't in our textbook. That was when I realized that learning and living don't have to come from a hierarchical system, and these institutions don't really have all the answers. That started opening me up to wondering what else was I not aware of. What else was outside the parameters of what I could discuss? That set me on the path of looking outside mainstream viewpoints on life.

My Insight

What insight did you have as a result and how did that change your life?

I realized there was a difference between 'learning it' and 'living it.' Learning it was trying to figure out the potential solution to every possible failure that I may make in life, and waiting until I thought I was old enough or qualified enough or learned enough so that *then* I could live it. *Living it* was just starting before I was ready. I discovered that all the greatest contributors to society where people who started before they were ready – when they were 'too young,' or 'not qualified yet,' or 'not experienced enough,' or scared, or didn't have the solutions. So I discovered that most of living comes when we are uncertain.

I realized that my routine brought me a level of security – I played college basketball and went to school every day – but although I had comfort and confidence, that didn't mean I had freedom. Freedom is often birthed out of uncertainty, and so I quit school and college basketball and I traveled around the world without a map. I put myself into uncomfortable and unusual circumstances, at times without money, always in Third World countries where I couldn't even speak the language and stood out like a sore thumb at 6 foot-four inches tall. I found that the more I could put myself in these uncomfortable situations, the more life was opening to me, until I ultimately fell off a cliff in Indonesia and my whole life flashed before my eyes. That was when I realized that there was no place in space or time I could travel to that would fulfill me. I would become fulfilled when I shared my gifts with the world. I also realized that my gift was sharing my story of stepping out of the prescribed lifestyle of society.

So I came back and wrote my first book *Into The Wind*, and everything has kind of taken off from there. I just sent in my new book, *The Purpose Principles*, which is being published by Penguin Random House next year, and I had the opportunity to give a TED talk; we are creating the film script right now for my first book, and we're working on putting a TV show together with one of the producers from *American Idol*. All of these things just started happening once I took those initial steps into complete uncertainty. Also, I'm believing that something greater than myself will provide for me, and if it doesn't then I'm working as hard as I can to get there. And I'd probably say that when you choose to live life for yourself, everything is given to you. And not many things are given to us when we are living life for other people if we don't really know what we want. It's hard to get what we want if we don't know what we want because we are living according to what somebody else, or something else, or the media tells us we want, or our parents want for us, or what our institutions or government want from us. And if we're living that way it's hard to get what we want.

If we know what we want and we create clear goals and write it down, then we make it happen, then we experience what we want. That's taking the initiative to do those things, and I think most of us never take initiative in our life because initiative requires stepping into uncertainty. When you take the initiative toward something you don't know, what's going to happen? We are so used to being inside certainty, to knowing what's going to happen: the alarm goes off at 6:30, then I'm going to be in traffic for 22 minutes, and I can eat my eggs in traffic and drink my coffee then, and I know for the next six hours that I'm going to be getting paid for the amount of work that I'm putting into this job, and then I'm going to come back about 5:30 and I'm going to catch 40 minutes of the news; then I'm going to drink a glass of wine, and then I'm going to make my dinner and then I'm going to have about three hours to relax and maybe read a book on my Kindle. We become accustomed to comfort. And if we're stuck in certainty, then we can never experience uncertainty, and uncertainty is where surprises come in, and new gifts come in. So perhaps it's because I've taken initiative to step into uncertainty.

My Message

What message would you like to leave with the reader?

It's what Jack Canfield told me. I once asked him, "Jack, what's the most important thing everyone on earth needs to know?" He replied, "Write it down and make it happen." And I looked at him, waiting for him to say something else. He could tell that his answer wasn't enough for me, but he said, "That's it. If you have a desire for something, then you also have the ability to make it a reality, because you would never have had the desire in the first place had it not been possible."

So writing things down and getting clear about really asking ourselves – you know, making a list of about 30 things you want to do or have, and then taking steps toward those is what I would invite people to consider. The beautiful thing about that isn't that you're going to get to a certain place in space and time, or achieve a certain thing, but what you'll uncover about yourself: the characteristics that you have to develop, the discipline that you have to develop, the habits that you have to hone. That progress of character is, I think, how we measure fulfillment, so I think that setting clear goals and then developing ourselves in the process is really how we can become fulfilled. That's what I would offer to people.

Bio

At the young age of nineteen, California surfer Jake Ducey dropped out of college, left behind a drug-filled life, and went in search of deeper meaning. His quest led him on a life-changing journey that has resulted in his debut book **Into the Wind: My Six-Month Journey Wandering the World for Life's Purpose** *(Waterside Press), released April 2013. Upon return from his spiritual adventure he raised the funds to build a school and home in San Marcos, near Lake Atitlán in Guatemala to support orphans who are taken care of by a Quiché Maya Shaman. Jake's profound transformation from a college dropout and drug addict to an inspirational author and motivational speaker had led him into social and environmental activism, including a three-day unlawful detainment for protesting the Keystone XL Oil Pipeline. He has since formed the non-profit organization, The Self Reliance Institute (a 501 C3), devoted to providing essential resources and opportunities for young people to become more self-reliant. He is a contributing author to* **The Rise** *by NY Times bestselling author Greg S. Reid. A certified yoga instructor, poet, and lyricist, Jake is determined to share his empowering messages to ignite and inspire a new generation of truth-seekers.*

Jake's website: www.jakeducey.com.

James Wanless

My Tale

Was there a particular event or experience that was a turning point in your life and somehow changed your view of the nature of reality?

Yes, in my case it was dramatic and traumatic. I used to be a professor of political science. I have a PhD from Columbia University and I was teaching political science in the Middle East – in Cairo and in Beirut. I was doing fine, even voted "professor of the year," so I was very popular and it was cool... but. And this was a big "but" in the sense of asking myself, *this is it?* I couldn't believe that going to one of the highest realms of academia was giving me the wisdom I needed to live my life. I felt somewhat unfulfilled and incomplete, and I knew there was more.

Meditation had always interested me, and I had played around a little bit with TM (Transcendental Meditation) and got my magic mantra. And I really kind of liked it, but I didn't go very deep. So I was meditating, but my inner voice, my intuition, told me when I was teaching in Beirut, "Go east, go east." Intuition is great, but you have to believe and trust in that inner voice. So I quit teaching and decided I was going to India.

I took the overland bus – this was the old hippie dippy days, the early 70s – going through Pakistan, Afghanistan, all the 'stans' and eventually ended up in India. I immediately decided to go to Nepal, to Kathmandu, because I knew it was trekking season. This was the season to go and walk in some of those great snow mountains, which sounded intriguing, but in Kathmandu I came down with hepatitis. And all of a sudden I couldn't even walk. All I could do was sit around and lie around, and I got all yellow – I was sick! I've never been a go-to-the-doctor kind of person, so I thought maybe I'll just wait this out. While I was lying in bed in this lodging, someone told me that there was a meditation course going on for Westerners at a Tibetan Buddhist monastery just outside Kathmandu. I thought, well I want to learn how to meditate and all I can do is lie around anyway, so sign me up. I struggled to get to this monastery, I had to walk for an hour or two, but I finally got there and began this month-long course for Westerners on Tibetan Buddhist meditation. It meant waking up at 4 o'clock in the morning and starting our full-on meditations at 4:30 am, and doing the whole Tibetan Buddhist routine.

Every day we would meditate and I would fill up my body with a golden Buddha light, and run it through my body and into my liver where I thought my hepatitis was probably centered, and we'd transmit it to the world. We'd do this for hours and hours every day, along with all the other kinds of ritual, which is really a kind of *son et lumiére* extravaganza. There were mudras and chants, incense and full body prostrations to the Lama, and all this kind of mojo – it was pretty spectacular really. After 30 days of meditating there I walked out of that monastery with no hepatitis. I never took any medication and my political science career was over. I was fully on the spiritual path.

I went all over India following other teachers of meditation. That just changed my life totally, dramatically. I'd been a left-brained, brainiac professor, and now I was more of a right-brained, whole brain, intuitive brain, kind of seeker, if you will. So, I went from an authority, a seer in a sense, to a seeker after the meaning of life and higher states of consciousness. Ultimately, that's how I got to be talking with you today.

My Insight

What insight did you have as a result and how did that affect what you do now?

My world, up until then, had been kind of a linear world: A leads to B leads to C – a very straightforward, rational way of looking at how the world operates. But from that experience in the monastery I realized that the world is not like that. It is a lot more holistic, and everything is connected and very strange and synchronistic. Everything depends on everything else, so the world is far more magical, far more mysterious, far more inexplicable than I would have ever thought as a political science authority.

The problem with being a seeker on the spiritual path is that you still have to pay the rent. So when I came back to America after another year or two of travel in the Far East, I had to find a way to make a living. I started teaching Eastern meditation practices and philosophy in San Francisco at small institutes. But then I had a tarot reading once with a wonderful shamanic teacher, Angeles Arrien, and I was so totally turned on I took a class with her. I thought this has great mojo, this was magic, I love this and I can do this. This is very empowering for people and I can touch them with this tool. So I just started becoming a professional tarot reader, to the horror of all of my friends and my parents. Of course, they thought I was totally bonkers, and maybe I was, because I pretty much starved that first year.

It is true that if you follow your bliss the money will follow, but you don't know when! So here I was in my little office, doing a few readings a week and teaching a class or two, but it didn't make any difference about the money because I loved it so much. I was really turned on by it in my mind, heart, body and soul. Still, after a couple of years of doing classic tarot, I became bored. I thought, *enough of this old world of medieval stuff. Let's take the wonderful structure of the tarot, these universal principles of life as a map of consciousness, but update the map! Let's get it out of 16th century Europe with all these white people playing around as knights with swords, with blood and kings and queens, and take it into the 21st century as a multicultural map of the human psyche.*

I started working with an artist friend of mine. I'd take my images from my garage to his garage, and we'd collage these 78 Voyager tarot cards together: after four years we had this deck.

Then it got published and I was off and flying, so here I am today.

My Message

What message would you like to leave with the reader?

That we are so much greater in a multidimensional way than we would ever think. The beauty of the tarot is that we are truly multidimensional; we are all these archetypes, from lovers to hermits, from magicians to fool, from priestess to Emperor. These are inner characters, and we need to access them and realize them in our lives to live our destiny, which is to be all that we can be – all that we are meant to be. And that's my message. Come on, get with the program! Grow yourself. Reach your apotheosis. Live up to your highest potential, accessing all the different parts of yourself.

Bio

James Wanless, PhD was a distinguished university professor in the Middle East when he experienced a life-threatening disease, which led to a spiritual transformation. He relinquished his academic career and began to share his newfound wisdom and inspiration.

James is a futurist and pioneer of new thinking, and recognized for weaving timeless wisdom into modern life with intuitive tools and symbolic systems. With his magical blend of personal charisma, humor and pragmatic enthusiasm, he is thought of as a "corporate shaman" and an internationally known authority on intuition.

He lectures, trains and consults throughout the world. He is the noted creator of the best-selling modern classic, **Voyager Tarot** *(250,000 sold to date) and also the author of* **Way of the Great Oracle; Strategic Intuition for the 21st Century; New Age Tarot;** *and* **Wheel of Tarot**.

James Wanless has often been called "Mr. Tarot" or the "Tarot Revolutionary" because of his enormous contribution to the field of tarot. James is a master tarot reader with over 30 years experience. Dr.

Wanless, educator, has created online courses in Tarot – Way of the Seeker (a personal growth path) and Way of the Seer (reader's certification). He has also developed a groundbreaking technique for using the tarot as a proactive tool for Fortune Creation and Life Coaching.

His latest book, **Intuition @ Work***, and his work with organizations, corporations and individuals regarding the "Intuitive Imperative" can be found on his websites, in his Intuition @ Work Audiobook, and in his Podcast series on iTunes entitled* **Intuition Into Action***.*

Dr. Wanless has also created a forthcoming new deck called **Sustainability Cards** *for using nature as a model and set of inspiring principles for personal sustainability and success. A natural Green Man, he is the author of the classic,* **Little Stone: Your Friend for Life***.*

James' website: www.jamesmwanless.com

JD Messinger

My Tale

Was there a particular experience or event that somehow changed your view of the nature of reality and was a turning point in your life?

Yes, I broke my neck in a submarine accident in 1985, and my neck had healed. But by 1999 it was deteriorating again, and on the morning of January 18, 2000, I put my arms in the air to stretch and the last thing that was holding my neck together snapped, twisted my spinal column around, and crushed the nerves. It felt like someone was splitting me in half with an axe, and the shocking part was that I left my body and became an observer of my body, which then looked like a ragdoll that had collapsed and flopped on the floor. I went through a tunnel, a gateway, and a wormhole. Those were amazing experiences that I did not remember for a long time. I had to restore my mental and physical body over a period of months first.

I was a left-brained nuclear engineer, an advanced math major with 12 years of reactor kinetics, physics, and metallurgy. I was a nuclear submarine officer, Exxon executive, Ernst and Young management consulting partner, and had so much left-brained business process technology in me that I used to say that I walked with a port list (a Navy term for leaning to the left). Then God, or the universe, broke my neck and straightened me out. So that was my wake-up call that caused me to question not only the nature of life and reality, but who I was and why I was here. It was my wake-up call to get me back on my path and fulfill what I came here to do.

During my recovery, as I lay on my bed staring at the plaster in the ceiling, I discovered that I had been living to work. I had no feeling in my arms, neck, and back, and I couldn't walk because they took bone out of my hip to repair my neck, so I was pretty depressed. In addition to all the trials and tribulations of physical recovery, I discovered that I wasn't happy in my life and I wanted to know why. I realized that I had been so busy working, that I didn't stop to live.

Lying in bed at home, in my frustration I prayed to God and asked, "Why did you do this to me?" My three-year-old son came into the room less than three minutes later and said, "Daddy, you work too hard." The next day I said another silent prayer, "Well, God, if I work too hard what do I need to do?" A couple of minutes later the door handle jiggled and in comes little Grant, who said, "Daddy, you need to play." Skeptical mathematician that I was, I calculated the probability of this happening, and it was one in 1 million that it would've happened. So the third day I said another prayer, feeling a little bit better. I said, "Oh, I worked too hard and need to play. Can you give me a straight answer?" Sure enough, the door handle jiggles and in comes Grant and he's bouncing around on his toes, and says, "Remember, remember, remember, remember!"

The probability of Grant answering three silent prayers in a row in less than three minutes was one in a billion, so that was another aspect of my wake-up call, the realization that God could really answer my prayers through my son.

My Insight

What insight did you have as a result and how did that affect what you do now?

The first insight, at the mundane level, was that I realized who I was and that I was not what I did – my job or my title. I realized that money didn't make me happy, that I was living to work instead of working to live; that I was detached from all of the things that were most important to me – my family – so that was a huge shift.

The second aspect was that it put me on a search to understand who am I, why am I here, and where did I come from. This ended up being a nearly 12-year quest, which I would call my spiritual awakening. I became consciously aware that reality was not just what I could see and touch. I discovered that we exist in a world of light; that I'm energy surrounded by billions of electromagnetic particles and my thoughts intermingle with other people's thoughts; that death isn't the end; and matter is not solid, and a whole bunch of other deep, philosophical kind of realizations. I had had so many strange experiences, visions, and insights about future events, like the energy crisis and the financial crisis. On a physical level, the vertebrae in my neck had also regenerated, where previously they had been solid, fused bone.

I had several original inventions that I was able to commercialize, which stemmed from visions or dreams and therefore made me to wonder about the source of the ideas. I launched a radio show on CNN called *Global Evolution*, and I interviewed Nobel laureates and thought leaders from around the world, asking them questions about time, life, living, genetics, and DNA. Can my thoughts reprogram and restructure my bones, and restore my vertebrae, I asked? And the short answer was yes. They said matter is not solid: it's pure energy and we can reprogram our stem cells and our DNA with the power of our thoughts.

I started studying the conscious, subconscious and unconscious mind, and how it all works. I learned that our brain is like a transducer and receiver on submarines, sending and receiving thoughts. I learned that our reality is the outcome of our intentions and motivations, which are the devices that set the thought process and tune the frequency of our transducer-receiver (i.e. our head) to open up to receiving guidance and insights. One of the most powerful things I discovered is that when you really let go of the outcome and attachments, when you let go of your pain or suffering from the past or your fears of the future and live in the now, as a cartel that would say, you begin to experience more of the totality of reality. You can see and experience insights and communications, and messages and signs.

One of the things that happened was that I wrote a book in eleven days: *11 Days in May*. When I was done my wife asked what the book was about, and I replied, "I don't know, I haven't read it yet." It was a book of 36 short parables that answered the great questions: Who am I? What am I? What is love? What is war? What is sex? What are thoughts? What are intentions, or matter? Very profound stuff! And I don't claim to be the author of the book; I am the scribe. I took the messages and I wrote them down, but it is a conversation between me and an un-named friend.

My Message

What message would you like to leave with the reader?

I think that there are lots of people who talk about healing, happiness, pain and suffering. Having been a transformational leader of large corporations across the globe, I can't help but look at the macro. But I think the micro situations, like putting fluoride in the water, the uncontrolled use of genetically modified organisms, the influence of corporations over politics – those are all micro manifestations of the macro situation, which is that we are exterminating ourselves. We have become consciously aware that we are interdependent and interconnected, sharing our thoughts, and the air we breathe, the water we drink and the food we eat. If we don't shift our rudder, if we don't move from this world of division and separation to one of cooperation and unity, we are in big trouble. The main message is to realize that what binds us together is greater than what separates us; to revive the values and virtues that made us great; to restore purpose and meaning; to restore moral capitalism; and to find more noble and ethical leaders out there to lead us through the 21st century.

Bio

JD Messinger is a best-selling author and futurist whose career began with service as a nuclear submarine officer in the navy. He later became an expert in all aspects of oil and energy, working for Exxon where he helped supervise the Valdez oil spill cleanup, and as CEO of Ernst & Young Consulting in Singapore. JD has been an advisor to Fortune 100 companies and members of government on five continents and had his own radio show on CNN. JD was one of 37 Distinguished Graduates from the United States Naval Academy at Annapolis. His book, **11 Days in May***, is the story of a remarkable spiritual experience that took him by surprise.*

In 2012, JD added another two accomplishments: an award winning and #1 best selling Amazon author, and his fourth Innovation of the Year award, this one for the world's first two-way interactive full emersion e-book. An international speaker, Messinger has been interviewed on dozens of television shows as a featured expert on innovation, crisis response, and the future of energy. Dignitaries and executives around the world have praised Messinger's thought leadership. His position papers on economic development, crisis response, and the future of energy have been distributed to numerous Presidential candidates, members of parliament, prime ministers, and royal family members in both the United States and abroad.

JD's website: www.jdmessinger.com

Jessica Maxwell

My Tale

Was there a particular event or experience that was a turning point in your life and somehow changed your view of the nature of reality?

Well indeed, and it was truly one I could not have imagined. I had never heard anything like it and in my case I had no context for a spiritual background of any sort, my mother having had a particularly bad Catholic girlhood experience that alienated her from religion. So I always tell people that when I talk about this event, you can take it to the bank.

What happened was that in 1992 my father died. Three days after he died I was driving by myself and I looked up at the sky and there was his face projected onto a very pure, cloud-free, plane of blue. It was his face, but his expression was one of a kind of joy unlike anything you experience or see on the earth plane. He was beyond euphoric, and so was I. I was also surprised because in life my father was an angst-filled, brilliant, but self-referential human being. He'd had a sad and lonely childhood and he was never very happy – I can't ever remember seeing him smile or hearing him laugh. So seeing him filled with this supernatural joy was unthinkable. And the kicker is that without having any spiritual interest or knowledge at all, I knew that some part of him still existed, even though his body had died, and he was now a lot happier. I knew that the ultimate message was that death is just fine.

After that I really didn't grieve his passage. But I wasn't about to tell anyone about this experience because, as so often happens, I was afraid people might think I was crazy. However, I was not allowed to keep this little secret to myself because my little sister called me that evening from 1,000 miles away to tell me that that day had been the most amazing day of her life, because, in her words, "I saw Daddy in a vision." "Wait, don't tell me," I said, wanting confirmation. "By any chance did you see his face in the sky, just beaming with joy?" And that's exactly what she had seen.

So now I had a witness and what I didn't know is that my third eye, as it's called in the East, or second sight in Scotland, had been blasted open. Thus did my spiritual life begin, and we were off to the cosmic races. That was the turning point of my going from a secular, disinterested, non-spiritual, very earthy, nature-loving, fly-fishing, adventure travel writer to becoming a spiritual adventurer for evermore.

My Insight

What insight did you have as a result and how did that affect what to do now?

Interestingly, I had always been amateurishly interested in quantum physics. Again, that was looking at weirder aspects of reality, but through the lens of science. So that was comfortable. But the experience of seeing my father's face conjured up the whole world of energy that you learn about when you study even the most basic principles of quantum physics. So, as they say, everyone's a skeptic until it happens to them. At that point I knew we were dealing with a part of everyday life that was deeper, stranger, and yet just as real as what we consider everyday life – in fact, it kind of felt more real. And I've often reflected that it's a good thing my interest in quantum physics gave me *some* basis in the actual strangeness of everyday reality as a context for the wild experience of seeing my dad's face in the sky.

You would have to be kind of asleep at the wheel not to ask questions like: "Okay, if my dad's spirit or energy field or whatever you want to call it still exists apart from his body, then what is reality? What is real? And if the experience of seeing his energy field or energy body was one of such incredible euphoria, then what does that say about the spirit?" Of course, the other, bigger part of this, which I wrote about in my spiritual memoir *Roll Around Heaven*, is that things are not only what we see. In fact, what we don't see may be even more important, and certainly rather more thrilling than what we do see. That presupposes that there is a whole parallel reality that seems to be embedded in this one, one just begging to be explored if you decide you want to go deep.

I was totally intrigued, but I didn't know what to do next or where to turn for answers. In short order, and without any conscious seeking or request for help, I met a spiritual teacher who happened to be a pig farmer. He took me on as a student and led me into the deep center of Christian mysticism and Eastern thought, and showed me where those bodies of work and understandings intersect. I drank it in. It was dizzying and exciting, and I only wanted to know more. Suddenly this whole concept of an energetic shadow world or inner world became very real. Once you cross that line you still have to make dinner and sleep and do the laundry, but you're living in two realities at once, ever aware of the deeper one. At the very, very least it makes life a lot more interesting.

My Message

What message would you like to leave with the reader?

We need to drop the term 'woo-woo' out of our spiritual lexicon because everything that denigrates the mystical is rooted in fear. The truth is, in our time we are accumulating evidence of the existence and nature of the quantum field, as well as the infinite nature of our own Spirits. It is a very thrilling time to be alive. I just say open your heart, open your mind, and step onto this bullet train to deep heaven – it is your birthright. Enjoy the ride. I tell people I'm not a believer: I'm a knower. And I know because of personal experience. Once you start saying yes, the world opens up and blooms like a flower and so do you. Sometimes there's a big 'kaboom,' but I also experience small miracles virtually every day. Everyone can – it may be the perfect solution to a vexing problem showing up in the most original way, or an Orb appearing just after you said something important – like a cosmic explanation point. One time I was making a client a cup of rooibos tea while telling her how hearts seem to follow me around, and we both looked down and saw that the tea in the tea strainer had made a heart shape! Everyday miracles, I think, are little valentines from the Divine to us, reminding us we're on the right path.

I will also add that you want to have a spiritual practice, because it's the only way – short of the very few human beings who get zapped with pixie dust and all of a sudden are fully awake like Eckhart Tolle. For the rest of us, maybe you get a wake-up call like I did, but then you have to do the work. And the work means suiting up and showing up every day for whatever practice you're drawn to do, whether it's meditation or prayer, or music or whatever. The energetic spiritual practices that we do literally create physical changes in our brains, which create the emotional triumphs we all want.

Every healthy human being wants to be happy. We want peace. And we want to be able to manifest what we really need in our lives, whether it's love or healing or purposeful work. Eventually, if you have patience, the personal miraculous becomes part of your personal reality. You simply do not want to miss this. There is no greater gift, reward or joy than authentic spiritual accomplishment, and you just have to do the work and love doing it and eventually the prizes will be yours – guaranteed.

Bio

Jessica Maxwell is the author of many books and articles on fly-fishing, adventure travel and golf. **Roll Around Heaven** *is her award-winning unbidden debut into the spiritual genre.*

Her work has been included in more than two-dozen anthologies, including Bill Bryson's **Best American Travel Writing 2000** *and Tim Cahill's* **Best American Travel Writing 2006**. *She was the youngest regular contributor to* Esquire's *Travel column, and created and wrote* Audubon's *in-the-field conservation column, "True Nature," and a definitive cover story for* Natural History *magazine on the plight of Pacific Northwest salmon. Her narrative, "Pride of the Norwegian Woods" (June 2007) was* Gourmet *magazine's first and only hunting story, and her November 2008* Gourmet *feature on Portland's restaurant scene was nominated for a James Beard food writing award.*

Today she maintains a lively energetic healing practice devoted to demystifying enlightenment and fast-forwarding her clients' spiritual progress by seeing and clearing lifetimes' worth of emotional trauma. Meanwhile, she remains one of the few female members of the Flyfisher's Club of Oregon. When she isn't leading private spiritual tours of Bhutan or out stalking Himalayan trout, Jessica lives in Western Oregon, with her trial attorney husband, Tom Andersen, where "we have a lot of fun correcting each other's grammar." As for **Roll Around Heaven**, *her best friend refers to the whole business as "Lucille Ball trips over God."*

Jessica's website: www.jessicamaxwell.com

Julia Assante, PhD

My Tale

Was there a particular event or experience that was a turning point in your life and somehow changed your view of the nature of reality?

Absolutely, I remember it very, very clearly. There were several of them in childhood, but the first major one, when I was about seven, was an experience with a tree – a large maple tree on our street. I was a very lonely child, and I often tried to talk to spirits – it must have been my Catholic upbringing, but also partly inner nature, so I tried to talk to angels or God or Jesus or whatever, and in this case it was this tree. And when I had embraced it, which I couldn't do wholly because it was a very large tree, I suddenly traveled up the tree – I was swept up in a kind of spiral into the sky. At that point I knew what infinity was. And I knew the ineffable feeling of divine love, because I was engulfed by it.

I always think of this experience as the infinity moment, that moment that rips all illusion away and lets you see that one hub of reality, that eternal truth of being. It was God-filled. I felt completely connected to all things and knew the experience was communication, a definite message. I was so overwhelmed with gratitude and wonder that I wept. It was just the recognition of this endless, simultaneous, great spacious moment. And I understood everything. It's as if at that point there was nothing more I needed to know.

Another remarkable event had to do with climbing into a cherry tree in full bloom. It was a spring day, one of those impossibly vibrant blue-sky spring days. I was lying fairly high up in the tree, staring up through the pink blossoms against the blue. I started to feel a kind of shimmering everywhere, as if another layer of reality were becoming palpable to me. It shimmered, and it was conscious. That was the thing. It knew me, it knew every single petal on that tree, it knew every speck of bark, and it knew everything in the universe. It held this all, with unimaginable compassion and love. And that's the first time I had direct contact with what I call "the Presence" – a divine manifestation, but not God. God, who I call All That Is, is way too big to manifest in such a way. Again, there was the feeling of being overwhelmed, and the sense of reality as we know it being ripped away to see what's underneath.

My Insight

What insight did you have as a result and how did that affect what you do now?

These intuitive revelations are still the basis of my belief in a benign universe, and I have experienced all of these things in much more extended forms since then. This experience of the Presence is uppermost in the afterworld when you have a good transition, or in a positive near-death experience, which I have had too. But it's also something that we can experience here and now. We feel it sometimes when we're just waking up in the morning – this deep, cozy, loving sense of safety. I went through a six-month period of living with the Presence every day. It was an extraordinary time of my life. I saw interdimensional beings all around me and had constant communication with other dimensions, or an inner reality or a greater reality, one might say. I was for once above the human drama, meaning above the drama that we humans make for ourselves, the scripts that we write for ourselves. I was completely above it, in that I was out of that human nexus. I saw the humor of it, the sadness, the tragedy of it, but still also how innocent it all was – even murder, even the worst crimes one can imagine, even the most horrible family stories – how deeply innocent it really all is. And that also has never left me. So then my attitude about human beings, about creation in general, is that at the foundation of all realities there exists this primal reality of beauty and good intentions. And when I work with people that's what I see in them.

Because of the book that I wrote, most people think of me as a medium, but I'm a very scientifically-oriented, research-oriented person. I like to combine the two. I'm not afraid of using analytic skills to analyze experiences or even terrains, like the so-called afterlife. I use academic skills in order to look at the evidence, or the stories that we have. I'm probably the only person who has studied the material that we have on the afterlife from the view of post-colonial theory, for instance. The intellectual side of me is very strong and helps to shape the intuitive side – they really work hand-in-hand. Most people believe that the intellect distorts intuition, which is not at all true. People who have this sort of belief miss so much.

My Message

What message you would like to leave with the reader?

My message is from some events that have happened in my life, extraordinary ones like meeting Yacob, or James, the brother of Jesus. He said, "Tell them, do not wait to die to be immortal." That means that we should operate from a perspective of immortality, one so much greater than what we have now. We should operate knowing that the transition from life to death is no more than a little switch in focus away from the material world. That's the big picture for me. Life goes on, it never stops. I'm never more dead than I am now, and I'm never more safe – and I will always be safe. And this I know.

Bio

*Julia Assante, author and scholar, is an established social historian of the ancient Near East. Yet for almost four decades she has also been an active professional intuitive. In her award-winning book, **The Last Frontier: Exploring the Afterlife and Transforming Our Fear of Death**, she applies the insights and methodologies gained from both fields in order to present a uniquely rigorous investigation of where we* *go after we die.*

From 1977 to the present Julia has been an active professional psychic and medium. In addition to private sessions, she teaches workshops on remote viewing, healing, reading the body, mind and superconscious, after-death communication, reincarnational recall past and future, and conscious dying in the US, Canada and Europe. She also coaches physicists, medical professionals, entertainers and athletes to develop specific career-related psychic skills, and assists the dying.

*In 1987, Julia was certified for practicing an especially effective type of regression therapy from AAPLE (LA), founded by Dr. Morris Netherton, work she continues today. She has been an ordained minister since 1985 of The New Seminary (NY), an Interfaith Seminary founded by Rabbi Joseph Gelberman and Sri Swami Satchidananda, where she taught for two years. In 1984, she participated in clinical tests on telepathy and remote viewing at Columbia University, resulting in accuracy scores high above other professional psychics. Her interest in religious beliefs and magical practices has been fed by decades of working alongside shamans, healers, and gurus from non-Western traditions as well as academic research of pre- and parabiblical religions (Mesopotamia, Egypt, Israel, Greece and Rome). She is now investigating ways a revolutionary medical device that operates on the level of quantum biology can be adapted to scientifically **prove** life after death.*

Julia Assante received her doctorate in Archaeology and Art History of the Ancient Near East from Columbia University. On invitation, she studied the cuneiform languages of Sumerian (the first known written language) and Akkadian (the first known Semitic language) at Yale. She taught at Columbia, Bryn Mawr and the University of Münster and excavated in Crete (Minoan levels) and Israel. She has given talks at major universities and conferences in the United States and Europe and has written numerous scholarly articles. Her breakthroughs in the interpretation of Mesopotamian magico-religious rites have provoked revisions in all scholarship of antiquity, including biblical studies.

Julia's website: www.juliaassante.com

KAYA

My Tale

Was there a particular event or experience that was a turning point in your life and somehow changed your view of the nature of reality?

Yes, there was one that really changed my life about 18 years ago. As an artist and a writer, I've always been involved with different foundations – I have a foundation myself, and I think it's really important to give back. So I received a call during that very intense period of my life from the Children's Wish Foundation with a request from a young woman. She was 19 years old and about to die from cancer, and she had a dream that she had to see me before she died. I took the first plane to visit her and I had one of the most profound afternoons of my entire life. We exchanged information, some of which is still secret inside my soul. Two weeks after that very spiritual and profound encounter, she passed away at 6 pm.

Without knowing that she had passed, she visited me that evening in a dream to thank me. She said she had a gift for me. She took my hand and brought me into a large room that had a table in it. In the table was a square like a large mirror, and through it I was able to see the tunnel of light that we see when we die. It was so beautiful – crystal blue colors that you never see here on earth. She said to me, "Normally you have to die to see this, but seeing this while you are alive, don't be shy. Talk about it."

I woke up with tears of joy, and this triggered inside of me a change that is still inside me today. Seeing that tunnel of light completely transformed my consciousness, and I started to receive 10 to 50 dreams per night.

I decided to walk away from fame and glory, and lived like a hermit for many, many years, to discover more parallel worlds, and dreams and signs. I started to work with the Angels and I discovered that an Angel is a metaphor to express the capacity of the human consciousness to dream and to travel in the multidimensions of life.

My Insight

What insight did you have as a result and how did that affect what you do now?

I was always very, very spiritual on my own, even as a young child, so when that experience started an awakening in me I was like a scientist, wanting to know more and more, discovering myself and trying to cleanse weaknesses and memories to improve myself and to grow. So now in my work, the notions of understanding symbolic language are one of the most profound and important keys for any spiritual personal path. I think symbolic language is the language of the Angels – God – and it brings us the capacity to have a concrete spiritual life. Because most of the time people are praying to God or the Angels – or whatever their tradition is – and it's always abstract. They do not receive really concrete answers until they discover spiritual symbolic language. So through that we can understand dreams and we can use the same symbolic language to interpret signs in our concrete life. And I've been teaching this now for so many years, traveling around the world. Thousands and thousands of my students have completely transformed their lives by knowing symbolic language. So when we open our angelic consciousness, we start to learn symbolic language and I think this is very important for future generations.

My Message

What message you would like to leave with the reader?

The main message is that you can become an angel. An angel is a metaphor for the human consciousness raised to an upper level that has the capacity to travel and learn in metaphysical worlds. I still continue to receive 10–15 dreams every night, so I continue to evolve. I have dreams about the past, present and future, and I can make better decisions, I can travel, I can help people and heal them in dreams. I can co-participate in the evolution of the universe and in God's work. With time and practice you can do it consciously. The more we cleanse our memories the more we raise our consciousness and become strong and very powerful.

I think that the most important message that I want to bring to humanity from the Angel Work and revelations that I have received is that we can all become angels, and that it is a natural process of evolution. And the more we develop into the consciousness, we develop clairvoyance, clairaudience, clairsentience: we become mediums and we have the capacity to receive information and to understand, through symbolic language, God's information. Then we have our wings and we become angels and we have no more physical limitations, because we understand also the major reason that we are here. Angelic Consciousness teaches us that we're here to develop the qualities that will let us become a better soul. That's the only purpose of our evolution in this world and everywhere in the universe. Those are the keys to human evolution, and everything we do and experience is only to develop qualities and to become better souls.

Bio

KAYA is a spiritual teacher, author, and international lecturer on angels and a worldwide specialist on the interpretation of dreams, signs and symbols in more than 43 countries. He is also the founder, chairman and CEO of Universe/City Mikaël (ucm) a multinational non-profit organization. His profound spiritual knowledge, expertise on dream, sign and symbol interpretation, his philanthropy, exemplary devotion, and humanitarian aid is a source of inspiration for millions of people on the planet.

His books include **Dictionary, Dreams-Signs-Symbols, The**

Source Code; The Book Of Angels: Dreams, Signs, Meditation – The Hidden Secrets; How To Read Signs; The Traditional Study Of Angels; How To Interpret Dreams & Signs; *and he has released a music CD album called* **Born Under the Star of Change.**

KAYA's websites: www.kayadreams.com

www.ucm.ca

Kingsley L. Dennis

My Tale

Was there a particular event or experience that was a turning point in your life and somehow changed your view of the nature of reality?

I'd like to think that I now have a conventional view of reality, and perhaps the consensus is the unconventional view. I'm not sure it was a rational journey at all. I think if I listened to rationality I probably wouldn't have arrived at where I am. But, saying that, my understanding of reality is that we only perceive a very thin sliver or slice of reality. So what we agree to be the consensus is an interpretation based on a minimum of senses. To give an example, my understanding and experience is that we don't originate thoughts within our head or brain. We actually receive thoughts externally and that the human brain acts as an antenna. So what this means is that reality is part of a whole field, a quantum field of intelligence, which exists in a nonlocal environment throughout our physical universe. Our physical universe is a secondary manifestation from a primary source of energy/consciousness.

So for me, consciousness is primary. All matter and physical manifestation is secondary, and therefore the human apparatus is a kind of deciphering mechanism that receives and interprets. What we receive is an aftereffect of primary reality. To gain access to reality is what I and others would call, "work on oneself." By working on oneself we can develop our perceptual faculties to receive and therefore interpret primary reality to a greater degree. So the journey throughout my life is one of working on myself to polish my perceptive apparatus, to receive a more or larger slice of reality and of the bigger picture.

The beginning is what I call the internal alarm clock. From earliest memories as a child of around 8 or 9 years, I always had a different take on the world. I used my imagination a lot. I had a sense that I was in contact with the world but also a nagging sense of 'this isn't it,' which took me on a personal quest and investigation. I call myself a traditional seeker, in that I've never had a one-moment, wow! epiphany. But I had this internal alarm clock, which drove me incessantly to try and find out the answers to this nagging internal feeling. That took me through more than 30 years of experiences and encounters, traveling and working on myself to arrive where I am. So that feeling has been with me from earliest memories, and that's what has driven me to travel and to seek.

My Insight

What insight did you have as a result and how did that affect what you do now?

I learned to trust my instinct, and that has driven me in different directions in different parts of my life. Examples of these are trigger moments when an instinct comes to me that I can no longer continue where I am. This has happened several times in several countries, such as Prague in the Czech Republic and Istanbul, Turkey. And just when I thought I was going to continue in that position my instinctual sense told me that I would not learn anything more, that I was treading water. So that instinct drove me to take decisions that may have seemed irrational, like changing countries and ending career paths, but it has always worked.

I refer to my present path as the perennial philosophy. What I've been seeking is the kinetic knowledge which has been at the heart of all the wisdom traditions. What I mean by kinetic is that it is no longer static or crystallized into an orthodoxy or human institution, that then no longer is able to transmit the living and modern contemporary version of that wisdom tradition. So I came to that in my early 20s through the Gurdjieff schools. I then made contact with what you might call a modern, contemporary version of Sufism; I studied under a Mevlevi master in Istanbul.

What I found was that the living streams of these traditions don't tend to stay with these names or categories, and so I have tried to follow the living essence. I have said to people that we are in a time where we have to make the new age the new normal.

I don't call myself a mystic, but I work to try to normalize what people may call mysticism or spiritual themes. I would call myself a spiritual person. I have met many way-showers or guides along the way but perhaps only two people whom I would call completed teachers.

My Message
What message would you like to leave with the reader?

My understanding is that the human species is an unfinished species. That alarm clock that I spoke of earlier is within each person, and it is up to each of us to pay attention and to begin the first step on that journey to completion. Not only do we have the alarm clock within each one of us, but we have the capacity. It is therefore the responsibility of each person to decide consciously if they wish to make that journey of self-evolution and self-development, which would open up perceptual faculties to have a completely different perspective on the world – a perspective which I would argue is the natural, organic understanding of humanity's place in the cosmos and its relationship to Truth and Primary reality. That's an evolutionary journey for each one of us. You don't have to be special to have those stirrings.

Many people are having the sense that something's not quite right, that there's more to it, to life. It's just, perhaps, that they either dismiss it or they don't follow it up. I think I'm very normal, and I try to put that across in all my work, that I'm not anything special or different from anyone else that I'm speaking to. It's just that I took it up, and I went with it.

Bio
Kingsley Dennis, PhD is an author, researcher, and sociologist. He is

the author of **Breaking the Spell: An Exploration of Human Perception** *(2013);* **New Revolutions for a Small Planet** *(2012);* **The Struggle for Your Mind** *(2012); and* **New Consciousness for a New World** *(2011). He is also the coauthor, with Ervin Laszlo, of* **Dawn of the Akashic Age** *(2013). Kingsley is co-founder of WorldShift International, which is a conscious evolution initiative that promotes and supports a world shift both externally within our current global systems, as well as internally on a personal level.*

Kingsley worked in the Sociology Department at Lancaster University, UK, and has authored numerous articles on social futures, technology, and conscious evolution. He currently lives in Andalusia, Spain and continues to research, write, travel, and grow his own vegetables.

Kingsley's website: www.kingsleydennis.com

Larry Dossey, MD

My Tale

Was there a particular event or experience that was a turning point in your life and somehow changed your view of the nature of reality?

During my first year of private medical practice I experienced a dream that left me shaken, and which showed me that the world worked in ways I had not been taught.

In the dream, Justin, the four-year-old son of one of my physician colleagues, was lying on his back on a table in a sterile exam room. A white-coated technician tried to place some sort of medical apparatus on his head. Justin went berserk – yelling, fighting, and trying to remove the gadget in spite of the technician's persistent efforts. At the head of the table stood one of Justin's parents, trying to calm him and lend support. The technician repeatedly tried to accomplish her task but failed, as Justin became increasingly upset. Exasperated, she threw up her hands and walked away.

I awoke in the gray morning light feeling as if I had been turned inside out emotionally. I felt as if this was the most vivid dream I'd ever experienced – profound, numinous, 'realer than real.' But in view of the dream's content, this made no sense. I did not understand why I felt so deeply moved. I thought about waking my wife and telling her about it, but decided against it. What sense would it make to her? We hardly knew Justin, having seen him only three or four times before.

I dressed and went to the hospital to make early-morning rounds. As the busy morning wore on, I forgot about the dream until the noon hour. Then, while lunching in the staff area with Justin's father, his wife entered the room holding Justin in her arms. The boy was visibly upset, with wet, unkempt hair and tears streaming down his face. Justin's mom explained to her husband that they had just come from the electroencephalography (EEG) laboratory, where the EEG technician had tried to perform a brain-wave test on the youngster. She prided herself on her ability to obtain EEG tracings in children, which can be a demanding task. Her record was virtually flawless – until she met Justin. After relating to her husband how her son had rebelled and foiled the test, Justin's mom left with the disconsolate boy in her arms. Her husband accompanied them out of the dining area and went to his office.

By this time the dream memory had returned. I was stunned. I had dreamed the sequence of events in almost exact detail before they happened. I went to see Justin's father in his office and asked him to share with me the events leading up to the aborted EEG.

Justin, he related, had developed a fever the day before, which was followed by a brief seizure. Although he was certain the seizure was due to the fever and not to a serious condition such as epilepsy or a brain tumor, he nonetheless called a neurologist for a consultation. The specialist was reassuring; nothing needed to be done immediately. He would arrange an appointment for the following day for a brain-wave test, just to make sure nothing else was going on. It was a simple procedure and the EEG technician, he said, had a special way with kids.

Could anyone else have known about these events? I asked. I wanted to know if someone could have leaked information to me that I might have forgotten, which could have influenced my dream. Of course not, Justin's dad said; no one knew except the immediate family and the neurologist.

Then I told my colleague about my dream. He realized in an instant that if my report were true, his orderly, predictable world had been suddenly rearranged. If one could know the future before it happened, our understanding of physical reality was seriously threatened. He sensed my disturbance as well. Our conversation turned silent as we contemplated the implications of these strange happenings. I turned, left his office, and closed the door behind me. I did not bring up the event with him again.

Within a week I dreamed two more times about events that occurred the next day, and that I could not possibly have known about ahead of time. Why had a cluster of precognitive dreams erupted, when I'd never experienced them before? It was as if the world had decided to reveal a new side of itself, for reasons I could not fathom.

In all three instances time seemed to be reversed, with effects appearing before their causes. Rationally I knew this could not happen. Time simply could not reverse itself and flow backward, carrying information into the present from a future that had not yet occurred. I wondered whether my mind could somehow have strayed from my body into the future, retrieving information about events that would later unfold. Both possibilities violated common sense and every ounce of my medical training. My consciousness was localized to my brain and to the present; *all* doctors knew that.

It was as if the universe, having delivered a message, had hung up the phone. It was now my job to make sense of it – if I could.

My Insight

What insight did you have as a result and how did that affect what you do now?

These and other experiences have sensitized me to nonlocal awareness – awareness that lies outside of space and time, awareness that is not confined to the here and now. Health and illness, clinics and hospitals, are prime stalking grounds for these phenomena. Yet we physicians have a tortured relationship with them. We are trained to honor evidence-based medicine, with its rigid algorithms and decision trees. This approach deliberately excludes hunches, intuition, premonitions, meaning, and other varieties of knowing that don't conform to reason and analysis. I believe, however, that to be alive is to know things nonlocally, outside the here and now. This capacity is our birthright. It comes factory installed, part of our original equipment.

In 1989 I introduced the term "nonlocal mind" in my book *Recovering the Soul*. I can find no earlier use of the term "nonlocal mind" in print in the English language. Fortunately, however, "nonlocal mind," "nonlocal awareness," "nonlocal consciousness," and similar terms are now quite common, but in 1989 it was quite a radical thing to talk about the mind as nonlocal. I felt the term was necessary simply because of the evolving evidence that consciousness behaves nonlocally – i.e., it manifests as if it is not localized or confined to specific points in space, such as the brain or body, and as if it is not localized to specific points in time, such as the present. A shorthand term for nonlocal, unbounded mind is *infinite* mind.

For over a hundred years research has accumulated in painstaking experiments that consciousness is not in a place in space and time. These experiments number in the thousands, and are the subject of many recent articles and books.

My Message

What message would you like to leave with the reader?

I'd like readers to realize, as I show in my recent book *One Mind*, that minds at some level are connected and unitary. If minds are nonlocal in space and time, they are unbounded. This implies that at some level they come together with other minds and form a collective or universal mind. Nobel physicist Erwin Schrödinger, whose wave equation lies at the heart of quantum physics, was interested in this possibility and believed it to be true. As he put it, "To divide or multiply consciousness is something meaningless. There is obviously only one alternative, namely the unification of minds or consciousness... [I]n truth there is only one mind."

The ethical implications are monumental. The nonlocal,

unbounded, collective, one-mind view of consciousness permits a revision of the Golden Rule, a version of which is found in all the world's major religions. Rather than saying, "Do unto others as you would have them do unto you," the Golden Rule becomes, "Be kind to others because in some sense they *are* you." Our fate as a species on this planet may depend on the degree to which we honor our oneness with one another and all other sentient creatures. This realization of our collective, unitary existence is an antidote to the epidemic greed and selfishness that threaten to engulf us, and which we must escape if we are to survive and thrive.

The most majestic contribution of nonlocal mind, however, is the restoration of the concept of immortality. A mind that is nonlocal in time is infinite in time, therefore immortal and eternal. This realization dwarfs the practical, health-related benefits of nonlocal consciousness. The fear of death and annihilation has caused more suffering throughout human history than all the physical diseases combined. Nonlocal mind is a way of transcending this fear and suffering through the realization that in some sense we are temporally infinite – unborn, incapable of death, eternal.

Bio

Larry Dossey, MD, is the author of twelve books on the role of consciousness and spirituality in health that have been translated into languages around the world. His most recent book, **One Mind: How Our Individual Mind Is Part of a Greater Consciousness and Why It Matters**, *shows that our consciousness is infinite, immortal, and one with all other minds.*

Larry's website: www.dosseydossey.com

Meg Blackburn Losey

My Tale

Was there a particular event or experience that was a turning point in your life and somehow changed your view of the nature of reality?

I have been having moments of 'challenged reality,' really since I came to the planet, but truly I think the epiphany came when I had what is called a 'dark night of the soul.' Over a two-week period, everything I had created in my life that I thought gave me value – that spoke of my success by relationships of all kinds – everything just fell apart. My partners were pushing me out of the business that I had started and that was doing phenomenally well. And I woke up on my friend's couch one morning because it didn't feel okay to go home. I just didn't have anywhere else to go that felt good. I woke up that morning and everybody had gone to work, and I was just crying my heart out and I don't know why. I think I was just releasing a lot of pent-up grief.

I said to myself, "I'm not getting up off this couch until I get it – whatever that means." So I started to look at each one of those falling apart situations, and I came to two realizations very quickly. One was that I didn't like me very much, and the other was that I had been living my life based on what I thought everyone wanted me to be or do, and I didn't even know what I wanted or who I was anymore. And so I looked up, and said to no one in particular, "Whoever I am, whatever this is, I accept."

And I said it so humbly and so full of grief – I had nothing left emotionally. I had no idea what I really meant until later. One of the things that I did to start out on my new quest was to learn to tell myself the truth, to find my authenticity, because I had lost it. And so I made a pact that no matter what happened I would tell myself the truth about it. I realized as I went about this truth pact that I lied to myself constantly, and how much we all do. And so after I got a little practice with that, I started taking that out into the world and speaking very truthfully to people, not from an angry place but just as matter of fact. And that was hard – wow, it was really hard. Over time I became what I call less defended, and I didn't have anything to cover up: I never had to look back. And as a result of that, my intuitive nature just began to blow wide open. There was nothing blocking it any more. I was relaxed in myself. Everything that was not true in my life fell away very quickly and I started to attract new and different people and situations. So I think that the moment in my life was when I woke up that morning in a sense of total loss and grief, and realized that I didn't have to live that way and that it was up to me to make that choice.

My Insight

What insight did you have as a result and how did that affect what you do now?

Holy cow! As I said, my intuitive nature really began to open up, and I had always had it: I had always 'known' things. I've had an uncanny sense of reading people since I can remember. But as I became more authentic, as I was less guarded, let down my self-defenses, and started letting my intuitive nature become whatever it was, I was hit by a series of cosmic two-by-fours. One day to the next and the next I could do something else and see something else. It was mind-blowing and I started to feel energy to the point where I thought my body was going to explode. I didn't know where to go to release any of it. I didn't know what to do so I started moving with music, just to try and find some comfort in myself. And as I did, I started to see energy as I worked with it. And I started to say out loud, "Somebody show me what to do!"

One day, all of a sudden, this being showed up in my living room. He seemed holographic in nature, he was shining; he was absolutely glorious. And he started to move with the energy a little bit differently, but very similar to what I had been doing. And as he did I saw the energy transform in color and intensity, and I started to mimic him. I began to understand in my body and around my body what was happening as the energy changed and shifted, and when I did that the experience opened up. The next thing I knew, I was experiencing other realities, as if I were in a cosmic room talking to somebody in the earthly world.

A succession of holographic beings appeared over time, and they taught me about creation and consciousness, and life and healing, and science... I can't even tell you all of it since I don't remember everything. There was so much of it. As a result, my IQ shot up. I was able to talk about things I hadn't even read about. I started to apply the work to people as a healing modality, and I saw heart defects disappear, I saw tumors go away, and I realized the immensity of what I was learning, and what I had agreed to step into when I said I accept. I was able to find not only my divine nature but the divine nature in everything and everyone else. And I continue today to live that, and I write about it, I teach it, and I continue to learn. You know, something I think is very important in all of this is we never know it all. And if we stay open instead of needing to know what or where or who or why, if we just stay open and do like I did and say "show me," then creation listens to those things. And turns around and gives us back exactly what we're looking for.

So the answers are there. We don't have to go anywhere to find them. And I think that's another one of the most valuable lessons I learned and that's it's all right here.

My Message

What message would you like to leave with the reader?

We are all perfect, whole beings of creation. We are created of all things, and all things are created of us, and because of that there is nothing or no one that can ever be lesser or greater than us. Each of us is an intricately woven aspect of the greater one.

Bio

Meg Blackburn Losey, PhD is a Master Healer, speaker, and teacher. She is an Ordained Minister in both Spiritual Science and Metaphysics, and holds a PhD in Holistic Life Coaching and a Doctoral Degree in Metaphysics. She has served as a consultant to Good Morning America *and* 20/20 *news, and her expertise in relation to issues of children of the consciousness evolution is greatly in demand.*

Dr. Meg is the author of soon to be released **The Children of Now Evolution***;* **Touching the Light***;* **The Secret History of Consciousness***;* **Parenting the Children of Now***; the international Best Seller,* **The Children of Now***;* **Conversations with the Children of Now***;* **Pyramids of Light: Awakening to Multidimensional Realities***; and the* **Online Messages** *which are distributed globally. She is also a contributing author to The Mysteries of 2012.*

Meg's website: www.spiritlite.com

Nina Brown

My Tale

Was there an event or experience that was a turning point in your life and somehow changed your view of the nature of reality?

Absolutely. I was creating a wellness center in Santa Fe, and we were looking for funding. It wasn't going very well. I knew the funding was out there, but there seemed to be a block. It was actually the suggestion of the individual who was going to be the main investor in our wellness center that I begin automatic writing in order to perhaps identify what the block was. Well, I've never done automatic writing and hardly knew what it was. I took a piece of paper and a pen and I sat down at the table, not knowing what to expect.

What came out on this piece of paper was absolutely stunning! The language, the words, the eloquence... Really, my writing style was nothing like that. So I began writing every day, and the writing got stronger and my belief got stronger. So that's how my journey began.

The next step that is interesting to recount is that the writings, after about a year, suggested that I go to Jackson Hole in Wyoming and (this is so incredible) create an electromagnetic super tunnel connecting Chaco Canyon in New Mexico with Stardreaming (stardreaming.org) in New Mexico, and I thought Yellowstone and also Alpha Centauri.

You know, believing something like that is not what the ego personality wants to do. It was trusting in something greater – this innate knowing inside of me that took me to Jackson Hole – and was probably one of the most pivotal times in my life. It's a long story, but in brief I was in the presence of a master, Tyberonn of Earth-Keeper (earth-keeper.com), and he seemed to under-stand that really it wasn't Yellowstone that I was to go to, it was Cathedral mountain in Jackson Hole, Wyoming. He gave me a Phi Vogel Crystal and said, "Point it at the mountain." And so I pointed it at the mountain, and I went out of my body. It was the beginning of a whole new way of being. Then he said, "I want to do a reading for you from Archangel Metatron." I was told that I was an ascended master, and that I was on the planet to upshift human DNA, and on and on and on it went. Really what I want to share with you, which is even more of a turning point for me, was the shift from the ego personality to the acceptance of myself as a divine human.

Archangel Metatron could tell me over and over again that I was an ascended master, but what do you do with that information? Here I am a grandmother. Here I am someone who was formerly trying to put together a wellness center. Here I am a woman who was a former debutante in Philadelphia. I don't think I even knew at the time what an ascended master was, and I certainly didn't know what DNA was, nor upshifting it. I had no clue!

Time went on and my inner voices began to teach me how to do all the things that had been suggested, and I was even encouraged to write a book. Well, I could not publish that book – absolutely could not publish that book because I didn't have the internalization of myself as an ascended master. It felt like I was a hypocrite! It felt like I was speaking braggadociously. I almost pushed the red button instead of the green button, and I declared to the universe, no no, no – I can't do this! And then came the tipping point for me, which I'll describe as the shifting of the information to that of 'I am a divine human;' that I am a walking master, I am an ascended master. When I say "I," I mean more than me. Through the integration and the acceptance of this, I know this is my truth. It happened when St. Germain invited me on summer solstice, 2010 – that was the year that I was going to publish my book. He invited me to go to Mount Shasta, California, and of course I said, "Yes." When I was in Mt. Shasta, I went into lucid dream state on summer solstice, and I saw myself entering the chambers of the Cosmic Counsel of

Light. I had been told that my higher self, Anaya Ra, was a member of that Council. I saw myself walking into a chamber. I saw my higher self in front of me. I went up to my Anaya Ra, and we merged.

The next day, I was sitting on the ledge of Mount Shasta looking out over the panorama, and I knew without a doubt that behind me was this same being, this higher self Anaya Ra. And it merged into me and that was even more remarkable, because it was the higher vibration choosing to merge with the lower vibration being – the Nina, the ego. It was at that moment precisely that I knew without a doubt that I am a walking master. That I am absolutely an ascended master, and that I could, without any trouble whatsoever, publish my book. I could change all the hidden language in the book, which was covering up my identity because I was embarrassed. I used that wonderful computer function – search, find, replace – and removed all the disguised descriptions of myself as the author, and I publicly, openly used my name, Nina Brown.

So it was a turning point in my life, moving from the identity of grandmother, Santa Fe citizen, daughter and debutante – all of those ego personality identities – to the enormity of who we all are. I use the word 'me,' and it sounds so central-focused, but it is all of us. So this experience that happened for me, and about which I speak and write, is to be a model for others because we are each of us an individual aspect of All That Is.

My Insight

What insight did you have as a result and how did that affect what you do now?

Well, if you remember, the title of my first book was *Return of Love to Planet Earth: Memoir of a Reluctant Visionary*, and I was reluctant, no doubt about it. When I went to Jackson Hole, I did all of those things I wrote about in the book, but I did it from a reluctant perspective thinking that my identity was Nina. And now, I stand tall in my shoes, and I know the wholeness of who I am. I know that I am very much more than the physical expression of Nina. I am, like you, like everyone who will be reading this book, an individual aspect of All That Is. I am a divine human. So I speak it with confidence, I stand firmly in that knowing, and it's totally integrated into my being-ness.

My Message

Is there a message you would like to leave with the reader?

Absolutely. There is a question that I ask almost immediately when I am in session with someone, or when someone gives me permission. That question is so simple and yet so complex. The question is, "Who are you?" And the answer to that question is what I believe brings suffering and grief to so many people, or joy, ease, and grace. If we answer the question as "I'm Nina, I'm an author, I'm a lecturer," then the ego personality is struggling to preserve the survival of that identity. It is too small: too small! So the message is that we are divine humans. With this new paradigm, with this new 26,000-year cycle, let us move into the acceptance of that knowing, the integration of "I Am a divine human." And at that point we become sovereign beings. And that is who we are in my truth. You, the readers, are sovereign beings, authors of your reality, and responsible for it. And we each, individually and collectively, as sovereign beings, are the creators of the new ways of being on Earth and what I call the Golden Age of Divine Love. We cannot do that if we answered the question with "I am Nina." I am a sovereign being, author of my reality and responsible for it.

Bio

Nina is a cum laude graduate of Bryn Mawr College, and retired from the company she formed to assist women entrepreneurs. She has distinguished herself as a pioneer in business. In 1995, she was appointed by President William Clinton to represent him at the White House

Conference on Small Business and, the next year, was chosen as a Charter Member of Pennsylvania's Best 50 Women in Business.

During this time, speaking engagements included: the US House of Representatives Field Hearings, the Pennsylvania Department of Commerce, the League of Cities Women's Caucus, Wharton Executive MBA Reunion, and as the keynote speaker for the Entrepreneurial Women's Expo.

From there, Nina acted as a consultant and leader in the field of alternative medicine, collaborating to form a company to bring neurosensory diagnostic tools to injured veterans, who suffered brain impairment in the Gulf War and Vietnam.

Nina's book is called, **Return of Love to Planet Earth: Memoir of a Reluctant Visionary**. *Her most recent book is* **S.T.A.R.: A Now State of Mind**.

Nina's website: www.ninabrown33.com

Paul Chappell

My Tale

Was there a particular event or experience that became a turning point in your life and somehow changed your view of the nature of reality?

There were several events. I grew up in the South, and my mother was Korean and my father was half-white and half-black. I didn't fit in anywhere and was bullied. Actually, my friends now think I am a really cool racial mixture, but this is a new reality that only exists today because of the civil rights movement. I couldn't imagine that growing up, and I know my father couldn't have imagined that Americans would have that kind of attitude toward race.

My father was born in 1925 and he had grown up under segregation. Since childhood my parents always told me that the only place in America where a black man had a fair chance was in the Army. That was my father's reality, and this was a reality for a lot of black men. He had served in the army in the Korean and Vietnam wars, and had a lot of post-traumatic stress from war trauma. When I was around four years old my father attacked me in the middle of the night. He said he was going to kill me, and my mother had to bear hug him to stop him. It was terrifying to see this person, who I trusted and had been my protector, come apart. That was one of the initial catalysts that pushed me down the road to peace.

I went to West Point and served in the Army in Iraq. When I decided to leave the Army my mother started screaming at me. She said, "Are you crazy? Are you out of your mind? No one is going to give you a job or hire you. It's bad enough that you're Asian but you're also part black!" But I thought that if attitudes could change so dramatically about race, why can't we change attitudes about war, environmental destruction and so many other issues that affect people? We still have a long way to go on the road to peace, but if we have made progress, why can't we make more progress?

My Insight

What insight did you have as a result and how did that affect what you do now?

I was the only Asian boy in my class and I got picked on a lot in school. That's given me a lot of empathy for people who are bullied, who look different, people who feel like outcasts or are disrespected or mistreated. I realized that I could use my own suffering as a way to grow my empathy, and transform all that trauma and pain into greater compassion and understanding. Before, I used to really hate the suffering I'd been through, but then I began to see that if I use it to build empathy then it has a purpose.

I wouldn't take back that experience if I could, because if that hadn't happened to me I don't think I'd have much empathy today. That has become a life philosophy for me, to use all these painful things from my past to become a more compassionate human being.

During my Army service, I began to realize that humanity's greatest enemy is not a group of people in a far-off country. Humanity's greatest enemy is war. That realization came from West Point teaching me that war is a terrible thing that should be avoided. But West Point also teaches that war is basically a necessary evil – it's terrible but occasionally you have to do it. But when I studied nonviolence and waging peace I realized that it's like penicillin: we have alternatives to war, just as doctors today have alternatives to amputation. There are other things that they can do like curing an infection that could make amputation not necessary. So I realized that the power of waging peace, the power of nonviolence in the 21st century is far stronger than war – than the power of waging war.

I saw how Gandhi and King were strategic geniuses. They had

all the strategic thinking – even more strategic thinking than Napoleon, Alexander the Great, and Julius Caesar. Gandhi and King really appealed to my strategic mindset, in terms of military strategy, and even referred to themselves as warriors. Gandhi said, "I am a soldier, but I am a soldier of peace." And that's another thing that really appealed to me.

I joined the military truly wanting to make our country safe, as I think a lot of soldiers do, but I realized that with our immense ability to kill and destroy each other, nonviolence is the most effective way to make our country and planet safe in the 21st century. I want to shatter commonly held stereotypes about soldiers and peace activists. These stereotypes not only deceive and divide us, but they also prevent us from understanding the art of waging peace and the power it gives us to solve our national and global problems.

My Message

What message would you like to leave with the reader?

The message I'd like to leave is that the survival of humanity does not depend today upon our ability to wage war but upon our willingness to wage peace. The fate of our country, the fate of our democracy, our fate, and the fate of our planet, depend not upon violence but upon nonviolence. We have to begin to see nonviolence as something that we need for survival. If you look at all the major human problems that we have now – war, terrorism, environmental destruction, poverty, economic imbalances – none of them can be solved by any single country, nor can they be solved through violence.

It takes courage to pursue the path of nonviolence. We must teach nonviolence the same way that students learn math and history. The skills needed for waging peace are all just basic life skills: how to resolve conflict, how to have more empathy, how to live peacefully with people, how to calm ourselves and other people down, how to build our courage and overcome adversity.

If we do not learn these basic life skills we won't survive. I hope everybody will do what they can to practice the art of waging peace in their lives, in their communities and to use those tools and make our country and planet better as well.

Bio

Paul K. Chappell grew up in Alabama, the son of a Korean mother and a half-black and half-white father, who fought in the Korean and Vietnam Wars. After Paul graduated from West Point he was deployed to Baghdad. He rose to the rank of captain and left active duty in November 2009. The author of four books, he lectures throughout the country and internationally, and teaches college courses and workshops on Peace Leadership. He serves as the peace leadership director for the Nuclear Age Peace Foundation whose mission is to abolish nuclear weapons and to empower peace leaders.

Paul sees himself as living proof that nonviolent struggles such as the civil rights movement can create positive change, and he has dedicated his life to unlocking the full potential of strategic nonviolence. His books include **Peaceful Revolution: How We Can Create the Future Needed for Humanity's Survival** *and* **The Art of Waging Peace: A Strategic Approach to Improving Our Lives and the World**.

Paul's website: www.paulkchappell.com

Paul Von Ward

My Tale

Was there a particular event or experience that was a turning point in your life and somehow changed your view of the nature of reality?

Well I've had many turning points, but I don't know that there is a particular one in terms of my sense of reality, which has evolved over all these years. I started off, as most of us do, very naïve about the world and everything that seems to be reality. I had no great expectations as a child. My wonderful mother married a sharecropper farmer near a very rural town, and I was conceived near the end of the Great Depression. A fundamentalist Christian church played a big part of my life growing up.

When I was 12 years old I was 'saved.' I thought I was going to be a minister and save the heathen in Africa. But I moved away from that notion very quickly when it occurred to me to ask what kind of God would send all of those people in Africa to hell, when they hadn't even heard Jesus' message yet. It didn't make sense to me, but I stayed in the church anyway and was eventually ordained as a minister. I began preaching and doing revivals for young people, and when Billy Graham came to town we helped him set up his event. I was caught up in this culture, but another part of me was saying this is not the way – it doesn't all fit together. Paul Tillich came to Florida State University while I was wrestling with the notion of God. I said to him, "You're using the word God in another way." And he replied, "God is whatever you make it to be." To have someone of his reputation say that was a big turning point for me.

I dropped out of the church where I was a pastor and focused on my graduate program in clinical psychology, but once again that wasn't the right track. This was the beginning of the war in Vietnam, and when JFK (whom I had met as a young congressional intern) made his "Ask not..." speech, with a Master's degree in hand, I was commissioned as a naval officer. I eventually realized I wasn't a fit for the bureaucratic Navy, although I was on the list to command one of the PCF swift boats in the Mekong Delta. I had decided that I really wanted a more broad scope in my career, and was let go by the Navy to join the Foreign Service. I spent fifteen years as a diplomat that offered an opportunity to live and work at a very high level in society, learning other languages and being immersed in other cultures. It was another kind of turning point. When you go to India, Southeast Asia, and the Middle East, you begin to realize that the Christian orientation such as I'd had in the United States is limited, and that none of us has the whole story. I left fundamentalist religions at that point, looking for what I would call something like "universal natural spirituality."

The Foreign Service was a wonderful experience, but I became very frustrated about the management of the State Department by people like Henry Kissinger. While in the State Department I received a second Master's degree – in public administration at Harvard. I wrote a significant paper about the managerial problems in the State Department, challenging the establishment. It was published as a chapter in an anthology produced by some Harvard colleagues. That was my goodbye to government service.

I then expanded that chapter into a book called *Dismantling the Pyramid*, which analyzed the bureaucratic model of government, with all of the lobbying among the corporations, Congress, and the administration. All of this was designed to benefit themselves. So I started a nonprofit organization to promote cross-cultural understanding, peace, and cooperation among countries that were in conflict. I started projects with the Soviet Union and China and other countries to bring professionals and educators together for discussions and cooperative projects.

By this time I knew that I was on an inner-directed trajectory, but I wasn't clear what it was about. I had started out in the ministry and religion, and then I went into education and psychology, and then the military, and then the international political and governmental areas. And now here I was, working outside of all of these institutions at a nonprofit. By that time, and it was the first time I had really thought about it in these terms, I was thinking that maybe I'm recapitulating past lives in some sort of trail of reincarnations. I began to explore that, which got me into the arena of consciousness, spirituality, and new science.

I started exploring all of these areas while I was still heading my nonprofit. What drove me was much deeper and more powerful than curiosity. It was becoming my *raison d'être*. It was at that point that I understood the reason for all of those other experiences – from the sharecropper's shack and Northwest Florida through the capitals of the world and educational institutions of renown, experiencing cultures and religions that were different and evolving – making their contributions to humanity's cultural and intellectual development.

My Insight

What insight did you have as a result and how did that affect what you do now?

Some people would say I quit work and started working on my hobby of going to conferences and writing books and articles – an after-your-career kind of life. But in truth, this work is what I came here to do. All of these other stages were preparation – a sort of review of previous learning when I started writing about cosmology in *Our Solarian Legacy* and *God, Genes and Consciousness*, and about the world that we're in and how it is dysfunctional in so many ways. I think we need to understand why we have such conflict in the world. How is it that we have so many people who are not realizing their potential because of distractions, economic problems, and health problems? And I began to grow toward this point where I believe that the whole universe is a self-evolving, self-actualizing organism with its purpose being the evolution of consciousness in all species and beyond.

I arrived at this cosmology of a self-learning universe because it appears consciousness is foundational to all the other aspects, like energy and matter with which the universe creates itself. We humans are part of that process, which is a self-conscious evolution towards our inherent potential, a potential we are nowhere near realizing at this point.

My Message

What message would you like to leave with the reader?

Well, I go back to the earlier comment I made that my seemingly jumbled together careers don't make sense unless you see, or assume, a self-learning, self-correcting process that is neither physical and nor cultural. It's something that we bring to a particular lifetime accumulated through many, many lifetimes, and with the help of a lot of other beings in this and other dimensions. Try to understand the threads that get woven back and forth connecting us all. Let's get over the barriers separating us, and bring back a level of mutual learning and mutual support.

To use a Navy metaphor, we are all steering a course from day-to-day, and even though we may not know the final destination we must fix our gaze on the horizon, take our best guess, and head for the stars.

Bio

Paul Von Ward, born in 1939 on a sharecropper's farm, grew up in post-WW II Florida where he graduated (Phi Beta Kappa) from Florida State University – then earned two Master's degrees, at FSU and Harvard. Trained in psychology and ordained as a Baptist minister, he became a US naval officer in the Vietnam era and was then appointed a US diplomat by President Johnson. Following 18 years public service overseas and in Washington, DC, he resigned to found an international nonprofit dedicated to cross-cultural understanding and cooperation. He became a leader in the citizen-diplomacy movement leading to Gorbachev's perestroika policies in the former USSR and private American bridges to China and other nations.

Paul's most recent books, **Children Of A Living Universe** *(2014) and* **We've Never Been Alone: A History of Extraterrestrial Intervention** *(2011), reframe the current human story of our origins, the basis of supernatural religions, the institutions of kingship and theocratic governments, and provide plausible explanations of our genetic evolution. They explain the basis of previous and present cultural and religious wars. They expose the reasons why science has failed to incorporate the possibility of other conscious/intelligent beings who have and continue to interact with humans.*

His first book, **Dismantling the Pyramid** *(of government), in 1981 added to the Washington debate on government reform. His multifaceted career and continuing education prepared him to become an interdisciplinary cosmologist and prolific, independent scholar. He has combined current science in many disciplines to develop a "self-learning cosmology" to explain the universe's evolution, including humans. His work encompasses the possibility of nonhuman influences on the history of human development. His book* **The Soul Genome: Science and Reincarnation** *(2008) is the first comprehensive scientific analysis of the many areas of empirical evidence that support the concept of reincarnation.*

Living in the hills of north Georgia, he also writes articles and lectures in the US and abroad.

Paul's websites: www.vonward.com
www.reincarnationexperiment.org

Penney Peirce

My Tale

Was there a particular event or experience that was a turning point in your life and somehow changed your view of the nature of reality?

There were many experiences, actually, one leading to the next and the next. Mine was a gradual process of opening, with many strands of insights weaving together over time into a big braid. Everything expanded me. I was initially unaware of these insights in my teens. When I think back on it now there seemed to be a strong underlying purposefulness to the focus of my interests and attention. I began reading about psychic things then, and started writing poetry and drawing, which I think opened my right brain and kept it open to intuition.

Once, when I was in art school, one of my professors showed us how to draw negative spaces, so instead of sketching the leaves on the trees you draw the spaces between the leaves. I had never looked at the world like that, and it opened me to a new kind of perception. I was always curious about the mysteries and perception, and was a voracious reader of everything from psychic discoveries behind the Iron Curtain, to Fritz Perls and transpersonal psychology, to Alan Watts and the people exploring altered states of consciousness.

I didn't feel like religion alone was the path for me – it was too codified. I wanted a direct, more mystical experience of the higher reality so I could decide about spirituality for myself. So I ended up amalgamating many kinds of teachings: religious, shamanic, scientific, cross-cultural, and even the ancient mysteries from Egypt and the Essenes – I made a big stew. Then I studied clairvoyance development, learning to meditate and work with visualization. Doing the exercises, getting symbols and doing readings for people, then discovering that what I saw was accurate, was a phenomenal experience! I saw that I was good at it. At the same time, I began to interpret my dreams; I hadn't realized I was having fairly sophisticated precognitive and teaching dreams until then. I had many visions that were to guide me in the coming years, which fueled my love of seeing through the surface to find inner realities. So the clairvoyance training really changed me – I realized I didn't have to work in a corporation (I was an art director and graphic designer at the time), that I could make a living doing this sort of work.

I had a constant sense that there was just so much more to learn, so many mysteries that all fit together, if I could just see the overall puzzle. Studying metaphysics became the thing for me. I could look into the inner world to see what was causing the outer world. That principle made sense to me, and that's what has kept me fascinated. Look at the outside circumstances of a person's life and see what caused them; look at a mental illness and see what caused that; look at the way an event occurs and the forces underlying that.

My Insight

What insight did you have as a result and how did that affect what you do now?

It showed me that the nature of reality is such that there is a nonphysical, inner world that's very, very real. It is the world of energy, consciousness, and imagination – the imaginal realm – where everything exists and there is no limitation. That fuels the physical world, and we can have as much as we want if we can get rid of the clutter in the way – all the limitations, the negative thinking and fear that says we can't do and have what gives us joy. That became a primary way of thinking for me so I set out to clear my own fear, and identify the ideas I had taken on from others that actually weren't mine. And really, it took many, many years of clearing myself. I was very disciplined and probably not too easy to live with back then! And of course, it's an ongoing endeavor.

In the early years as I was opening, there was a lot of political unrest, freethinking, and opening into idealism. The more I thought about idealism, the more I sensed it was just the memory of the purity of spirit. I was always very idealistic and wouldn't settle for just anything. When I would compare an ordinary job with doing something I felt was real and truthful for me, I couldn't compromise. I zigzagged forward, moving from one thing to another, trying to get closer and closer to something that felt like the core of being – the most real thing. That got me deeper and deeper into the underlying principles of life – the universal laws governing how life works, how consciousness works. I really wanted to live from those truths.

My Message

What message would you like to leave with the reader?

I'm very positive about the transformation process we're all experiencing, and I do think that's what's underway today. I think we're shifting out of an old way of perceiving the world, and that old, linear perception has actually created the world we know and the way it functions. We're now entering a new kind of perception that will create a very different reality. And that reality is going to be fantastic! It's this new perception that I've been writing and talking about, and I think entering it fully is absolutely do-able in our lifetime. We just need to learn the steps and stages in the process, and be committed to choosing how we really want to feel, to living in the soul-in-the-body state, or what I've called our "home frequency." We mustn't allow negative thinking to dissuade us. I think our transformation and the world's transformation will unfold easily when we do these few basic things.

Also, I want to say that it's fine to be a little bit selfish. Don't give up on what you want to do and what you feel is right just because someone else doesn't like it or you think you're supposed to fit in with society. Just keep on being selfish (but not egotistical) and go for what feels right. I did that and didn't fit in with other people for much of my life, but it was probably the only way I could have gotten to my life's work. And now I feel connected to everyone! Growing up in the Midwest, none of this existed – the idea of becoming a professional intuitive was laughable or too outrageous to even imagine. But I was guided, by my own instinct coming from some higher level of Self, to stubbornly follow the breadcrumb trail toward something I didn't know *could* exist. It was a matter of gauging the difference between what felt just right and not quite so right. Anyone can do it: just pay attention.

Bio

Penney Peirce is a respected visionary and clairvoyant empath. She is known for her pioneering work in intuition development and her common-sense approach to spirituality and the development of expanded human capacities. A popular lecturer, counselor, and trainer, Peirce specializes in intuition development, "skillful perception," and dreamwork. Since 1977, she has counseled tens of thousands of individuals worldwide about life and business direction, and the fulfillment of destiny. Her clients include coaches, psychologists, scientists, and leaders in business, government, and the entertainment industry. She also advises other intuitives and trendsetters in the human potential movement.

Peirce's work emphasizes the practical aspects of intuitive development, helping people apply 'direct knowing' to increase natural efficiency and their enjoyment and participation in life. She teaches that life functions according to innate natural principles, and when we live in alignment with these truths, things work smoothly and effectively. Her work assists people and organizations in uncovering their purpose and action plan, understanding and easing transitions, alleviating burnout, and finding accurate answers to pressing questions.

Penney is the author of six books, including her "transformation trilogy," comprised of **Leap of Perception***;* **Frequency***; and* **The Intuitive Way***.*

Penney's website: www.penneypeirce.com

Peter Russell

My Tale

Was there a particular event or experience that was a turning point in your life and somehow changed your view of the nature of reality?

For me there wasn't a single turning point. I'm different from a lot of people there, I think. I always had an interest in other views of reality; even as a kid I was exploring things, and as a teenager I always felt there was something there, something different. I was at university studying mathematics and theoretical physics and that was the first time it really came to a head, and I discovered that nothing I had learned in mathematics and theoretical physics was going to explain why human beings were conscious in the first place. I was studying the Schrödinger's equation for hydrogen out of which the universe evolved, and the question I had was, "How come the universe had evolved into a being such as myself?" This was the great enigma: that I had the consciousness to study the universe.

When I realized physics wasn't going to help me learn the answers I started looking in other areas. I looked into philosophy, but that wasn't very helpful; I looked to psychology and then spent a year studying the brain, but no one there was interested in consciousness itself. And I realized that the people who were really interested in consciousness were the people who looked at consciousness firsthand. The secondhand way is using electrodes on the brain to see what's happening to the brain. But consciousness is a firsthand, subjective experience. And the people who studied consciousness firsthand were the spiritual adepts, the yogis, the mystics, the various people who sat down and observed their own consciousness through some meditative process or something similar.

So I started getting interested in meditation. That was the beginning of the shift, really. I learned various techniques, but found transcendental meditation really fascinating for me. It was opening up my mind to experiencing levels of consciousness that I hadn't known before in terms of noticing the internal quietness, and beginning to notice a deeper sense of self. So I followed that route and went to India and lived there for a while studying with the Maharishi and with other teachers. Two things happened in India, which I think really settled my life from then on. One was realizing there was something to spirituality. As a scientist I totally rejected religion. In fact, when I was 12 or 13 I decided it was a load of weird mumbo jumbo that didn't have any relevance to the scientific world we were living in. So I just completely rejected religion. I saw that religion was what happens to spirituality when you translated from one culture to another; over hundreds of years the essence gradually gets lost or distorted and absorbed by the culture of the time.

The other thing that happened in India was that I realized there was a common essence to all the world's spiritual traditions. They were all pointing in the same direction, although using different ideas and metaphors, but they were all pointing toward the fact that we live in a very limited mode of consciousness. It's really an egocentric, materialistic mode of consciousness based on the survival values of the physical organism. And that's where most people live their lives. This is what I think most spiritual teachers are pointing to, and the fact that this doesn't need to be the case. The whole of our culture was, in a way, looking in the wrong direction – outwardly rather than inwardly. We all want to be happy, basically, and at peace, but we're looking out there trying to get the world right, not recognizing that the source of peace is really inside us. So that realization was a major shift for me, and part of my life since then has been trying to distill the essence of the world's spiritual traditions into the core understandings behind them all, and putting that into very simple everyday language that the ordinary person, who is not interested in spirituality or religion, can understand.

My Insight

What insight did you have as a result and how did that affect what you do now?

I realized while I was in India that all the problems we were facing – from personal to social to ecological problems – all come back to human consciousness one way or another. They could be traced to poor decisions, to the wrong values, to shortsighted thinking, self-centeredness. And all the time we were looking out there to solve the problems by making new laws, and trying to control things, and stopping people from doing things. But we're not asking, "What is it in our consciousness that leads us off track in the first place?" I began to see that this is what the world's spiritual traditions had to offer: an understanding of how we get off track and how to bring ourselves back to ourselves. I think that became the motivation for me, for my whole life since then. Talking, running seminars, writing books, making films – it's all been about how to help people get in touch with essential spiritual teachings. I think this is the most valuable thing we can do in the world today.

Another shift happened, not in a single moment but as I continued with my understanding of physics and neurophysiology – I still love science and read a lot about it. Everybody was trying to understand how consciousness emerged from the brain, and they're still trying to understand this, but no one has any answers. It is one of the great enigmas of science: why are we conscious? And I realized that they had got it all back to front, that it was the other way around. Consciousness is always there. Being conscious is the one thing none of us can doubt. We can doubt almost everything else. Even right now we could be sitting in a virtual reality, and we'd still be conscious even though it all might be an illusion that we were experiencing. And that led me to the realization that consciousness is really fundamental to the universe. And that's something I've been continuing to explore ever since. Without realizing it, science is actually pointing to the fact that the fundamental nature of the universe must be more of the nature of mind, than of the nature of matter.

For the last 20 years, that has been an ongoing research of mine, just looking at what it means to say that consciousness is fundamental, rather than saying that matter and energy are fundamental.

My Message

What message would you like to leave with the reader?

I'd like to leave two. The first message – and this is something I realized over my whole exploration into the nature of consciousness and meditation – is that it is so much easier than we think. I think we put so much effort into meditation and trying to quiet the mind and get in touch with our deeper self. And more and more I see that it really boils down to just letting the mind relax, letting the attention relax. I think that's really all there is to it. It's just learning how to let the mind completely relax. And when we do so our thinking relaxes, our body relaxes, and we fall back into that natural state of consciousness, which is always there waiting to be touched.

And the second thing I would want to say can be summarized in two words: *be kind*. Be kind to each other, which, again, is one of the Universal teachings. It comes from the recognition that ultimately we all want the same thing. We all want to be respected, to be at peace; none of us wants to be rejected or to be trapped into suffering. But what we often do, though, is we try to manipulate other people by hurting them, often in very subtle ways. And the principle of kindness is recognizing that we are all of the same kind – we're all human beings looking for the same things.

In any interaction, consider this: *How can I interact with this person in terms of what I do or say to let him or her to feel respected, appreciated, and come out of this interaction feeling happier?* And when we start doing this in our relationships – our personal relationships, our work relationships, people we meet on the street – everything begins to change. A new form of love gets to come into our lives. That's what we're doing: we're caring for the well-being of another person.

Bio

Peter Russell is an author, public speaker, and multimedia producer who is recognized as a leading thinker on consciousness and contemporary spirituality. He coined the term "global brain" with his 1980s bestseller of the same name in which he predicted the Internet and the impact it would have on humanity. He is the author of nine books, including **The Global Brain Awakens; Waking Up in Time;** *and* **From Science to God: A Physicist's Journey into the Mystery of Consciousness.**

His principal interest is the inner challenges of the times we are passing through. Peter believes if we are to navigate our way safely through these turbulent times we need to listen to the wisdom of the world's spiritual traditions, as well as to our current scientific understanding.

Peter's website: www.peterrussell.com

Pim van Lommel

My Tale

Was there a particular event or experience that was a turning point in your life and somehow changed your view of the nature of reality?

I don't think it was a particular event. It was a number of events. I think the turning point, for me, was reading a book by George Ritchie called *Return from Tomorrow*. This book described his near-death experience as a medical student in 1943. He was declared dead for nine minutes, but regained consciousness after he got an injection of adrenaline right into his heart. He described an impressive near-death experience, and that was the reason I started to ask my patients who survived cardiac arrest – I'm a cardiologist – if they could remember something from their period of unconsciousness. Within two years I had asked 50 patients this question, and to my great surprise 12 of them told me about a near-death experience. It changed my view, and that was for me the start of my study of near-death experiences in survivors of cardiac arrest.

According to our current medical science, it is not possible to experience consciousness, let alone enhanced consciousness when you are unconscious and clinically dead. So that was the start for me, and talking to people with an NDE changed my view about both life and death.

My Insight

What insight did you have as a result and how did that affect what you do now?

People with an NDE were my greatest teachers, I would say. What they told me – and there were many, many hundreds of them, and thousands more wrote to me by e-mail – is that death is not death, and that there is a continuity of consciousness and everything is always connected – now and also when you're declared clinically dead. So there is always continuity. Consciousness is always without time or place, so it's non-local and it is not limited to the brain. So that was the main thing: that you change your view of life and death and about the mind-brain relationship.

I was very reluctant to accept it at first. I knew that it was not possible, and asked myself, "Well, how can we understand the possibility that people have this enhanced consciousness?" So for me it was scientific curiosity that started my study. I didn't have a personal experience, but I was very open and I could resonate with all those patients who wanted to share with me their near-death experience – which is actually a life-insight experience. It's all about love. It's all about unconditional love and compassion; first toward yourself, to accept yourself with your negative aspects, and then to love and accept other beings and also animals, nature and planet Earth. Because you are connected at another dimension; you are one consciousness: you are all one, always. So what you do to others you would do to yourself; what you do to planet Earth you are doing to yourself.

My Message

What message would you like to leave with the reader?

I'm very reluctant to call it a message, but rather what I learned from all those people. As a scientist, a cardiologist, I believe that science should be asking questions with an open mind. I'm also convinced that materialistic or reductionist science cannot tell anything about consciousness because you cannot prove it objectively, or reproduce the content of our consciousness. We cannot prove what we think or view. So, we need to change our science to include subjective experiences. I always tell people that he who has never changed his mind has never learned anything, so you have to be open to changing your mind if you want to learn something new.

And the other thing I've learned is that death, like birth,

presumably is just a changing state of consciousness. There is always a continuity. So it is not a message, it's just what I've learned.

Bio

Pim van Lommel, MD was a cardiologist in a large teaching hospital in Arnhem, the Netherlands, for 30 years and is now doing full-time research on the mind-brain relation. He published several articles on cardiology, and turned his research to near-death experiences (NDE) among survivors of cardiac arrest in 1986. He has authored over 20 articles, including a study on NDEs that was published in The Lancet *in 2001 which caused an international sensation, as it was the first scientifically rigorous study of this phenomenon.*

In his later articles he writes about his concept of the continuity of our consciousness, and about the relation between mind and brain. In 2005 he was awarded the Bruce Greyson Research Award on behalf of the IANDS (the International Association of Near-Death Studies) in the USA, and in 2006 the President of India awarded him the Lifetime Achievement Award at the World Congress on Clinical and Preventive Cardiology 2006 in New Delhi. Recently he received the 2010 Book Award from the British Scientific and Medical Network. His book **Eindeloos Bewustzijn** *(Endless Consciousness), released in English as* **Consciousness Beyond Life: The Science of the Near-Death Experience**, *became an international bestseller with more than 200,000 copies sold.*

Pim's website: www.consciousnessbeyondlife.com

Rajiv Parti, MD

My Tale

Was there a particular event or experience that was a turning point in your life and somehow changed your view of the nature of reality?

I had a personal experience in December 2010, on Christmas day, which changed my life forever. It was a near-death experience. After that I became a healthier and more peaceful person. My reality changed – how I view things at the personal level, spiritual level, and all other levels.

I was rushed to the hospital for emergency surgery because I had developed a severe infection after an implant from an earlier surgery. Doctors had to go in and clean out the infection completely. After anesthesia was induced, I saw myself floating in the operating room, about 10 or 12 feet high. At first I was surprised, thinking that maybe somebody had put some hallucinogenic drug in my anesthesia. But from there, my consciousness went to two different realms: first it went to the hellish realm and then it went to the spiritual, heavenly realm. There I met a light being who transmitted the understanding that everything would be okay, but that a lot of things would have to change in my life.

My Insight

What insight did you have as a result and how did that affect what you do now?

Before that experience my attitude was purely scientific and materialistic. Reality for me was only what you could see, feel, touch and smell – just the physical universe. I believed that consciousness was created by the brain as a byproduct of different chemical and analytical reactions within the brain. After this experience my perception of reality changed. I understood that consciousness exists outside the body, and that there is a spiritual world apart from the material world. I understood that there is a divine being whose essential nature is love.

This was very difficult to accept in the beginning, but since I had experienced it I had no choice but to accept. Things then started changing in my life without any effort on my part. Synchronistic things started happening that couldn't have been coincidences, and this made me believe it all the more.

My Message

What message would you like to leave with the reader?

The first message I would like to share is that wellness is defined on four levels – physical, mental, social and spiritual – and that social and spiritual wellness are just as important as physical and mental health and wellness. Spiritual wellness is connected to something higher than your own immediate ego. The reality of spiritual wellness is all love, all caring for other people and being rooted or grounded in the Divine Being.

Healing is also at all different levels. I had become addicted to pain medicines, and one of the things I discovered is that after this spiritually transformative experience changed my reality, my addiction went with it! I was now no longer addicted. My perspective had changed. Even Bill Wilson, one of the authors of the 12 Steps (of Alcoholics Anonymous) talks about having a spiritual experience as being one of the easiest ways to change your perception of reality – which really helps to overcome addiction. And I can report this from direct experience that forgiveness and love are equally important for healing, especially at the emotional and spiritual level.

I can summarize my message in three words: *forgive, love, and heal.*

Bio

Dr. Rajiv Parti is a world-leading specialist in pain management with over 30 years practicing clinical experience and 15 years as Chief of

*Anesthesiology at Bakersfield Heart Hospital in California, special-
izing in cardiac anesthesia. Dr. Parti founded the Pain Management
Institute of California, and under his direction it has treated thousands
of patients for acute and chronic pain relief.*

*In 2005, Dr. Parti personally encountered the first of a series of life-
threatening health challenges that led him to explore non-traditional,
evidence-based complementary and alternative medicine. Enduring
seven surgeries and ensuing complications over the next two years, Dr.
Parti was gifted with a near-death experience that showed him his true
purpose in this lifetime: to be a healer of the soul, especially diseases of
the soul, of the energy body, addiction, depression, chronic pain and
cancer. Dr. Parti shares his experience and insights through his books*
**The Soul of Wellness; The Laws of Wellness; The Four Pillars
of Happiness**, *as well as in his coaching and speaking engagements.*

Rajiv's website: www.drrajivparti.us

Ruth L. Miller, PhD

My Tale

Was there a particular event or experience that was a turning point in your life and somehow changed your view of the nature of reality?

Well, I had what I like to call a large wake-up call: I consider all terminal diagnoses wake-up calls. There I was, doing everything 'right': finishing my doctorate; being the best wife I knew how to be and the best mother. I had just been appointed director of a program at my former university and I had a wonderful consulting business. Unfortunately, I began to collapse emotionally and physically. Then someone came up to me at a Christmas party, and said, "Your husband is having an affair with so-and-so," and things deteriorated from that point on.

So I was operating in a world of systems and cybernetics, consulting as a program planner and futurist, but my body was saying, "Nope, not happening." It got to the point where I could not function at all and I was in a lot of pain. The doctors really had no idea what was going on, but what they did know was that the internal bleeding had to be stopped, that my hormones were all screwed up, and that I didn't have any adrenal function left.

About that time some friends introduced me to a guy in Portland who did mind-body healing. He was really able to help quite a bit, pointing out that there was a direct link between the physical symptoms I was having and the emotional turmoil I was going through. And he pointed me to a book that I would never have picked up off the shelf on my own. It's called *Emmanuel's Book*, a channeled book by Pat Rodegast, with a preface by Ram Dass.

The book's message was so clear, so loving. To shorten a long story, the book led me to other books and resources, especially around mind-body healing, and healing through the power of forgiveness. And so I developed a process for myself that began to eliminate the emotional basis for some of the physiological symptoms. I became physically stronger; and as I got stronger, I discovered more and more resources to support my healing process.

As it turned out, much of the material that I was finding – or that was finding me – was written by people called New Thought ministers, many of them in religious science. And one of the things that I learned during that time was to begin to trust an inner guidance, because obviously my intellect was not serving me very well.

I got stronger and healthier and was able to go back to work, but after two years and a major financial loss my body started to give out again. During the time I went through what is called the *dark night of the soul*. It was an amazing experience, like being in a spacesuit floating in space without being tethered to anything. I was in total darkness, where there is nothing to contact – no one, nowhere, no how – and that lasted literally three days.

My Insight

What insight did you have as a result and how did that affect what you do now?

Finally, I remembered the voice within that I had learned to honor during my healing process. I told myself *you're not hearing it now but maybe if you reach out for it, it will be there.* And lo and behold it was – not just a voice within but a presence surrounding and embracing me.

That's when I really got that the path of the intellect was no longer the way I could live. The message was clear: the path of the *spirit* had to be the way that I was to live. I had to give up being a consultant; I had to become a minister. As I began again to follow the inner guidance, I was directed by a powerful dream to a New Thought church in Beaverton, Oregon. Six months later, through a series of blessings, grace, and synchronicities, I was ordained as a New Thought minister.

That was 20 years ago, and I have just left a church I've served for six years. It's perfect because I now understand that I have 20 years of practice working from that spiritual aspect of being. Now I can go back into the intellect from this foundation and bring forward what is useful, and integrate the two in a new way.

My Message
What message you would like to leave with the reader?

Get clear about which voice in your head is telling you what, and follow the one that is feeling most light and loving and lovely – my version of 'follow your bliss.'

Bio

Dr. Miller served as Associate Professor and Director of the Cybernetic Systems Program at San Jose State University and as Director of Curriculum & Evaluation for Rogue Community College. She has led countless workshops on new paradigms, systems thinking and futures research, and has served as adjunct faculty at Antioch University-Seattle, Marylhurst University, Portland State University, as well as the Living Enrichment Center, and New West Seminary – receiving the highest evaluations for her classes.

She was ordained in the New Thought tradition and became the pastor of the LifeWays Center in Portland, Oregon, then interim Assistant at Unity of Beaverton and Associate Minister for the Unitarian Universalist Fellowship of Grants Pass, and finally, the Pastor of Unity by the Sea in Gleneden Beach, Oregon. She now works primarily with The Portal Center for Unifying Science, Psyche, and Spirit.

She has held board positions for many Oregon nonprofits, including Sustainable Urban Neighborhoods, RAIN, the Alliance for Social Change, Flexible Ways to Work, and The Ecotopia Project, and helped to found the New West Seminary, the Aspen Grove Peace Project, Peacebringers, the Institute for Sustainable Culture, and The Portal Center. She is also the editor of a series called **The Library of Hidden**

Knowledge *for Beyond Words/Simon & Schuster, which offers modernized versions of the wisdom of 19th century writers and teachers such as Ralph Waldo Emerson, Wallace Wattles, Charles Haanel, and James Allen.*

Ruth has authored and coauthored numerous books, including **Mary's Power; Make the World Go Away; Unveiling Your Hidden Power; Finding the Path;** *and* **The Paths of Power** *(Biography Series).*

Ruth's websites: www.rlmillerphd.com
www.theportalcenter.org

Suzanne Giesemann

My Tale

Was there an event or experience that was a turning point in your life and somehow changed your view of the nature of reality?

Yes, that would be when I was attending the class of a mediumship teacher as a journalist. I was writing her story, and she surprised me by calling me to the front of the classroom. She told me that there was a spirit-being present – a relative of someone in the class. She wanted me to see if I could attune to the consciousness of that spirit and see what I detected. I proceeded to 'bring through' information about this man/spirit whom I previously had no idea was even there. I knew how old he was when he died, what he died of, what kind of work he did, what his nickname was, and then I proceeded to describe his hobbies. I was completely stunned that I had the ability to tune in to someone on the other side: it convinced me that mediumship was real.

The reason I was there in the first place was that I had lost my stepdaughter when she was struck by lightning a few years earlier. At the time, my husband and I had gone to see a medium, hoping that what we had heard about the afterlife was true. That medium brought through such evidence from my stepdaughter that I went on to write a book about mediumship. I was in the process of writing a second book about another medium, and it was her class that I attended that day.

My Insight

What insight did you have as a result and how did that affect what you do now?

The insight I had was that consciousness exists along a continuum – it's like a spectrum of energy. In our human form we're limited to one end of the spectrum, which would be the lower end. The spectrum continues growing higher and higher, and so what I'm doing is allowing myself to tune in to the higher vibrations of those in spirit by raising my own vibration. I use methods such as meditation and prayer, and clearing energetic blockages in my own body, which allows me to vibrate at a higher level, so-to-speak. It really boils down to physics. It's all a matter of fine-tuning this antenna. I believe that we are all instruments and all have this antenna, but not everybody is as finely tuned as others may be.

I believe we are our greatest enemies when it comes to having new experiences and experiencing higher consciousness, because our belief system holds us back. Once I opened my mind to the belief that the spirit world existed and that I in fact could tune in to those on the other side myself, a whole new world opened up to me.

Having come out of the military, it was quite challenging for me to make that shift of consciousness because I was always brought up to believe that if you can't see it, hear it, touch it, etc. with your own physical senses, then it doesn't exist. I was very 'by the book': there had to be rules for everything, and I applied those rules. It's only since I opened my mind and stopped applying so many rules and being so rigid that a whole new world has opened up.

Even after giving over 650 readings, I still learn every day how much I limit myself with my own beliefs. Every time I peel back that belief system and get rid of limiting beliefs, my attunement with the other side improves.

My Message

What message would you like to leave with the reader?

There are many people who communicate with the other side, but I think there are even more skeptics. We overcome our skepticism by providing evidence that this greater reality exists. That's why I stress that I'm an evidential medium, because I came from that skeptical side. I was very by the book, and it is the preponderance of the evidence that has come through in my readings and in my dealings with those on the other side that has convinced me, and that has allowed others to believe that this life we see is not all there is. So if there's anything that I would want to get across it's the great importance of evidence, because my goal is to bring credibility to the work of mediumship, to communication with higher consciousness, and it's the evidence that does that.

Bio

Suzanne Giesemann is a former Navy Commander with a Master's degree in National Security Affairs. She served several distinguished tours including duty as a commanding officer, as a special assistant to the Chief of Naval Operations, and as aide to the Chairman of the Joint Chiefs of Staff, the nation's highest ranking officer.

It was the tragic death of Suzanne's stepdaughter that propelled her on the unexpected path to her current work. Since discovering her ability to communicate with the unseen world in 2008, she has given over 650 one-on-one evidential readings, providing comfort and healing to those who are grieving by bringing them verifiable evidence of the presence of their loved ones.

In addition to being a spiritual teacher and workshop presenter, Suzanne is the author of ten books. The story of her transition to her current work is told in her book, **Messages of Hope: The Metaphysical Memoir of a Most Unexpected Medium**.

Suzanne's website: www.LoveAtTheCenter.com.

About the Editors

Miriam Knight holds a BA and MA in Psychology and held senior positions in health and technology-based companies and institutions in the US, Israel and Europe. Upon returning to the US, Miriam published a holistic journal and founded *New Consciousness Review*, a review site for transformational books and films. She recently co-founded a speaker's bureau, *Luminary Voices*, for transformational speakers and musicians. She is also the host of an award-winning weekly interview show on Internet radio.

Julie Clayton is a freelance editor of *New York Times* bestsellers and award-winning books in the new consciousness genre. As an editorial consultant her clients include publishing houses, NGOs, academic institutions, and innovative global communities. Julie is the Reviews Editor for *New Consciousness Review* and has reviewed for *Publishers Weekly*. She holds a Master's degree in Consciousness Studies and is pursuing her doctorate in Metaphysical Science (MscD) with the University of Sedona. Julie is currently writing a book on conscious evolution. Julie's website: www.sacredwriting.com

BOOKS

O is a symbol of the world, of oneness and unity. In different cultures it also means the "eye," symbolizing knowledge and insight. We aim to publish books that are accessible, constructive and that challenge accepted opinion, both that of academia and the "moral majority."

Our books are available in all good English language bookstores worldwide. If you don't see the book on the shelves ask the bookstore to order it for you, quoting the ISBN number and title. Alternatively you can order online (all major online retail sites carry our titles) or contact the distributor in the relevant country, listed on the copyright page.

See our website **www.o-books.net** for a full list of over 500 titles, growing by 100 a year.

And tune in to myspiritradio.com for our book review radio show, hosted by June-Elleni Laine, where you can listen to the authors discussing their books.

MySpiritRadio